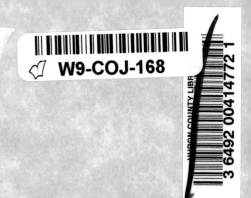

This book belongs to:

LEISURE ARTS, INC.
Little Rock, Arkansas

EDITORIAL STAFF

Vice President and Editor-in-Chief: Anne Van Wagner Childs. *Executive Director:* Sandra Graham Case. *Design Director:* Patricia Wallenfang Sowers. *Editorial Director:* Susan Frantz Wiles. *Publications Director:* Susan White Sullivan. *Creative Art Director:* Gloria Bearden. PRODUCTION — *Managing Editor:* Andrea Ahlen. *Project Coordinators:* Carol Bowie Gifford and Joyce Scott Holland. EDITORIAL — *Managing Editor:* Linda L. Trimble. *Senior Associate Editors:* Terri Leming Davidson and Susan McManus Johnson. *Associate Editors:* Shelby D. Brewer, Stacey Robertson Marshall, and Hope Turner. ART — *Book/Magazine Graphics Art Director:* Diane Thomas. *Senior Graphics Illustrator:* Guniz Jernigan. *Graphics Illustrators:* Faith R. Lloyd, Fred Bassett, and Linda Culp Calhoun. *Color Technician:* Mark Hawkins. *Photography Stylists:* Sondra Daniel, Ellen J. Clifton, Tiffany Huffman, Elizabeth Lackey, and Janna Laughlin. PROMOTIONS — *Managing Editor:* Alan Caudle. *Associate Editor:* Steven M. Cooper. *Designer:* Dale Rowett. *Art Director:* Linda Lovette Smart. *Publishing Systems Administrator:* Cindy Lumpkin. *Publishing Systems Assistants:* Myra Means and Chris Westenberger.

BUSINESS STAFF

Publisher: Rick Barton. *Vice President and General Manager:* Thomas L. Carlisle. *Vice President, Finance:* Tom Siebenmorgen. *Director of Corporate Planning and Development:* Laticia Mull Cornett. *Vice President, Retail Marketing:* Bob Humphrey. *Vice President, National Accounts:* Pam Stebbins. *Retail Marketing Director:* Margaret Sweetin. *General Merchandise Manager:* Cathy Laird. *Vice President, Operations:* Jim Dittrich. *Distribution Director:* Rob Thieme. *Retail Customer Service Manager:* Wanda Price. *Print Production Manager:* Fred F. Pruss.

CREDITS

PHOTOGRAPHY: Ken West, Larry Pennington, and Mark Mathews of Peerless Photography, Little Rock, Arkansas; and Jerry R. Davis of Jerry Davis Photography, Little Rock, Arkansas. COLOR SEPARATIONS: Magna IV Color Imaging of Little Rock, Arkansas. CUSTOM FRAMING: Nelda and Carlton Newby of Creative Framers, North Little Rock, Arkansas. PHOTOGRAPHY LOCATION: The home of Nancy Porter.

International Standard Book Number 1-57486-176-X

10 9 8 7 6 5 4 3 2 1

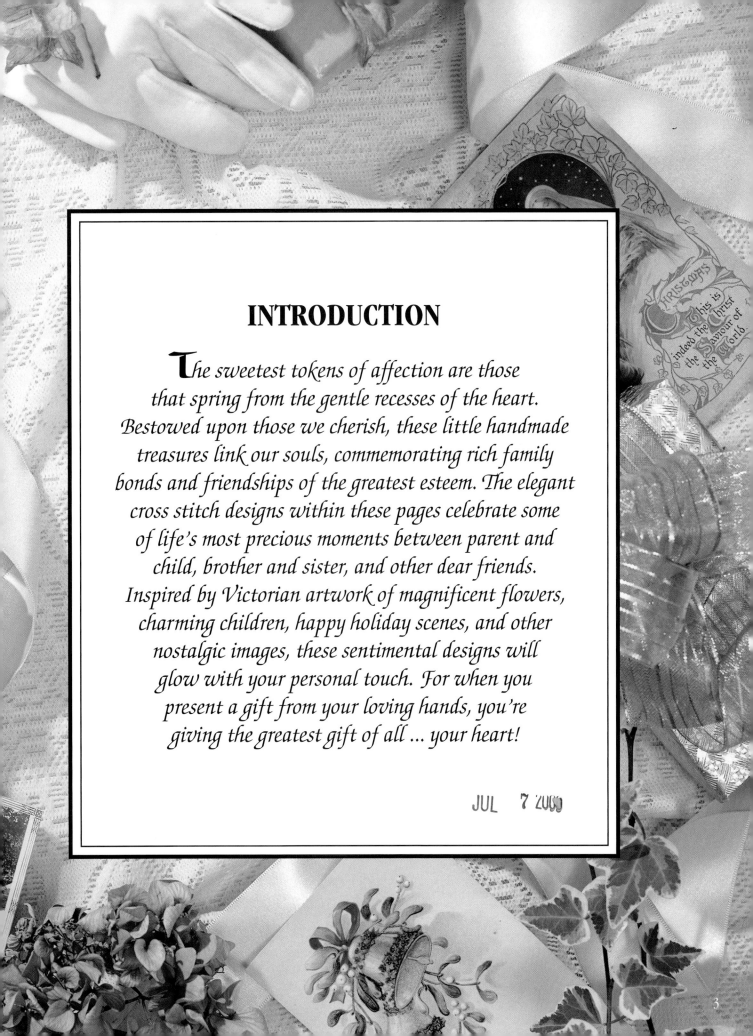

INTRODUCTION

The sweetest tokens of affection are those
that spring from the gentle recesses of the heart.
Bestowed upon those we cherish, these little handmade
treasures link our souls, commemorating rich family
bonds and friendships of the greatest esteem. The elegant
cross stitch designs within these pages celebrate some
of life's most precious moments between parent and
child, brother and sister, and other dear friends.
Inspired by Victorian artwork of magnificent flowers,
charming children, happy holiday scenes, and other
nostalgic images, these sentimental designs will
glow with your personal touch. For when you
present a gift from your loving hands, you're
giving the greatest gift of all ... your heart!

TABLE OF CONTENTS

4

BIRTHDAY BOUQUETS

Colorful bouquets bloom throughout the year within the pages of a loved one's heart. Pressed between the leaves of time, beautiful floral bookmarks will evoke the sweet fragrance of innocent dreams and delicate imagination. These tokens of love will bestow birthday wishes of inspiration and hope.

Charts on pages 44-47

7

DEAREST BABY

*T*he arrival of a child hearkens the
potential of the future, filling us with
a delightful sense of hope and expectancy
on the first of many birthdays to follow.
Tiny footprints capture the joyful moment
of a little one's birth. A treasure that
will be cherished both today and for years
to come, sentimental samplers display
the tiny joys of infancy on a pillow
or framed work.

Charts on pages 48-49

BLESSED WITH FRIENDS

What a blessing it is to have the friendship of someone who stands by you no matter what! That special person knows how to cheer you when you're blue, share a kind word of comfort when you're afraid, and lend an attentive ear when you're sad. For that forever friend, no other gift will do but one to touch her heart as she has touched your life.

Charts on pages 50-51

UNITED IN MATRIMONY

Something old, something new, something borrowed, something blue... With each budding flower, love springs anew. Preserve those moments of newly wedded bliss with heirloom samplers and accessories. Such remembrances preserve the eternal freshness of true love and anticipate the beauty of anniversaries to come.

United in
Holy Matrimony
Patricia Perry
and
Paul Wentzler

December 31
1994

Chart on pages 52-55

25th
Anniversary
Jessica
and
Thomas Smith
June 18
1975

Chart on pages 52-55

Chart on page 54

Within life's simplicities are found some of our greatest memories. The elegance of cross stitch combines with the soft caress of love and flowers to capture some of life's most cherished moments.

Chart on pages 52-55

SWEET HOLIDAY GREETINGS

All through the year, there are special days to remember. Love is in the air in February, just after the advent of the year has brought reflections on the old and hopes for the new. We observe faith-filled traditions, celebrate the birth of our country, greet fall, and mark the first Thanksgiving feast. Herald the arrival of each holiday with winsome pieces you'll cherish as much as the occasions they commemorate.

Charts on pages 57-59

An Irish lass costumed in her native green offers lucky shamrocks to one and all in honor of Saint Patrick's Day on a soft and elegant pillow. As the brisk winter gentles into balmy spring, Easter arrives with its message of rebirth, captured here in traditional pastel symbols of new life.

Chart on page 60

Easter
May the day for you
be filled with sunshine
and flowers and
friendly
greetings.

Chart on pages 62-63

19

*T*hank heaven for the seasonal celebrations
that bring us close to family and friends!
Independence Day often finds us settled
side by side on a blanket watching patriotic
bursts of color illuminate the warm July
night. When witches and ghosts come
prowling in late October, we shake
off our shivers of fright with spirited
laughter. Then, in the cool of November,
we gather to feast and give thanks
to the Lord for another year
spent with joy and great affection.

OUR UNCLE
He can't be beaten!

Chart on page 61

Chart on page 66

Chart on pages 64-65

CHRISTMAS OFFERINGS

As snowflakes collect on barren tree branches and cold nights invite cups of hot cocoa, a sense of goodwill in the air announces the arrival of the Christmas season. Sharing warm wishes of peace, hope, and love is one of the true joys of celebrating this magnificent holiday. It's a time for offering special thoughts and creating cherished memories with those we hold dear. Capture the feeling with an exquisite ornament, framed piece, and padded books featuring time-honored expressions for this most magical of seasons.

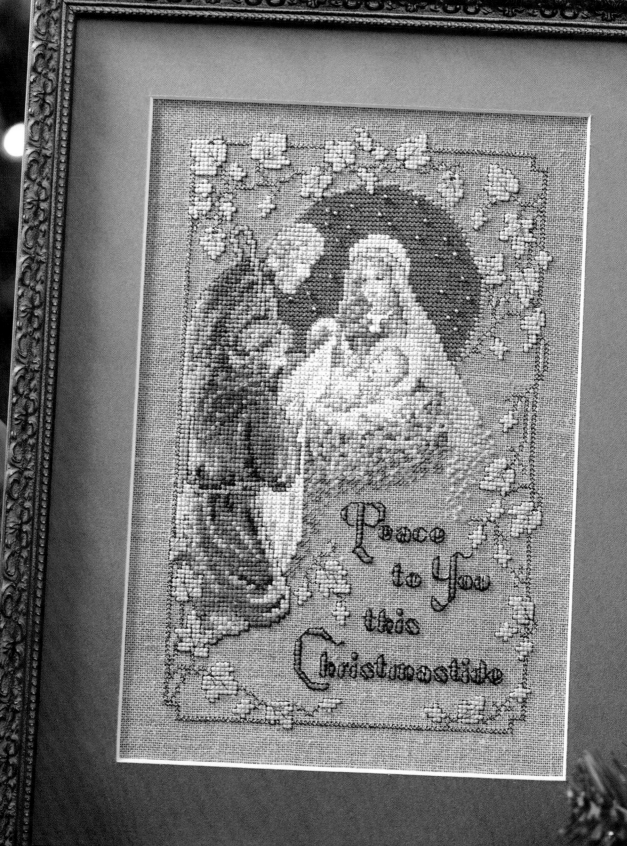

Peace
to You
this
Christmastide

Charts on pages 67-69

FOR WEE ONES

Acharming childhood classic, whimsical sock monkey adornments take us back to a place where carefree days were plentiful and possibilities were as endless as the imagination. Fun, friendly, and playful, many-splendored monkeys magically transform a child's room into a land full of laughter and glee — reminding us of the innocent joys of our youth.

Charts on pages 72 - 73

ANGELS KEEP THEE

Whether on earth or from high above, angels perpetually watch over us and those we hold dear. Their silent presence brings peace and tranquillity to everyone who truly believes in the power of love. Invite the heavenly hosts into your home with our glorious sampler, or choose one of the divine seraphs and stitch a pretty candle accent.

Chart on pages 74-75

VICTORIAN FANCIES

*G*listening *with the splendor of fine gems, garden glories and lacy touches beckon to all. These feminine fancies, which evoke the elegance of fine lace, are genteel accents for the boudoir. With refined ease, each display of beauty captures the essence of the Victorian age with all of its sentimental finery. Pleasing purples and perfect pinks adorn these stitched pieces, bringing their beauty into full bloom.*

Charts on pages 76-79

31

special people

By the sage advice of doting grandparents, the steadfast faith of mother and father, and the loving challenges of devoted siblings, we are shaped in the tender years of our youth. In turn, we invest ourselves in the lives and hearts of our children. Fashioned by caring hands, these lasting mementos will be daily reminders to all these special people of how very much they are loved.

A Mother's Love
Is Like A Garden
Where Flowers Sweetly Bloom
And The Path
That Passes Through Them
Gently Leads Us
Back To Home

Charts on pages 80-82

Chart on page 83

34

To see a boy working under his Daddy's gentle guidance or romping joyfully with his loyal dog is to be reminded of our own tenderly treasured childhood memories. These framed pieces beautifully capture the often unspoken but undeniably deep love between parent and child.

Chart on page 84

*They're so much more than just family ... they're your best friends!
Lavished with handmade love and nestled in a polished frame, these gifts are
meant to warm hearts twice: theirs in the receiving and yours in the giving!*

Charts on page 85

Chart on pages 86-87

CHERISHED MEMORIES

𝓔voking the sweet memories of distant days, cherished photos inspire reminiscences of moments past. Such nostalgic notions are showcased in these delicate displays of beauty and solemnity. A verdant vine encircles childhood memories while an ornate border encircles an angelic smile. Stitched in a tapestry of hues, these borders enhance the individual elegance nature has bestowed on loved ones.

Charts on pages 92-94

FRIENDSHIP TOKENS

$\mathcal{F}$riends are truly special people, warming our hearts with laughter and sharing with us the ups and downs of life. A long walk in the park beneath a clear blue sky or a quiet afternoon spent sipping tea with a friend can transform an ordinary day into a lifelong memory. Handmade offerings such as a delicate pansy sachet or a trio of lovely floral pillows are elegant reminders of just how dear she is to you.

Charts on pages 88-89

BASKETS OF JOY

*D*ainty accents for the sewing room combine the enchantment of needlework and garden pleasantries. Highlighted by pansies and violets, cradled blossoms and cuddly kittens capture the simple beauty of nature on a pillow, doily, and pincushion. Gather joy by the basketfuls with these notions of love and kindness.

Charts on pages 90-91

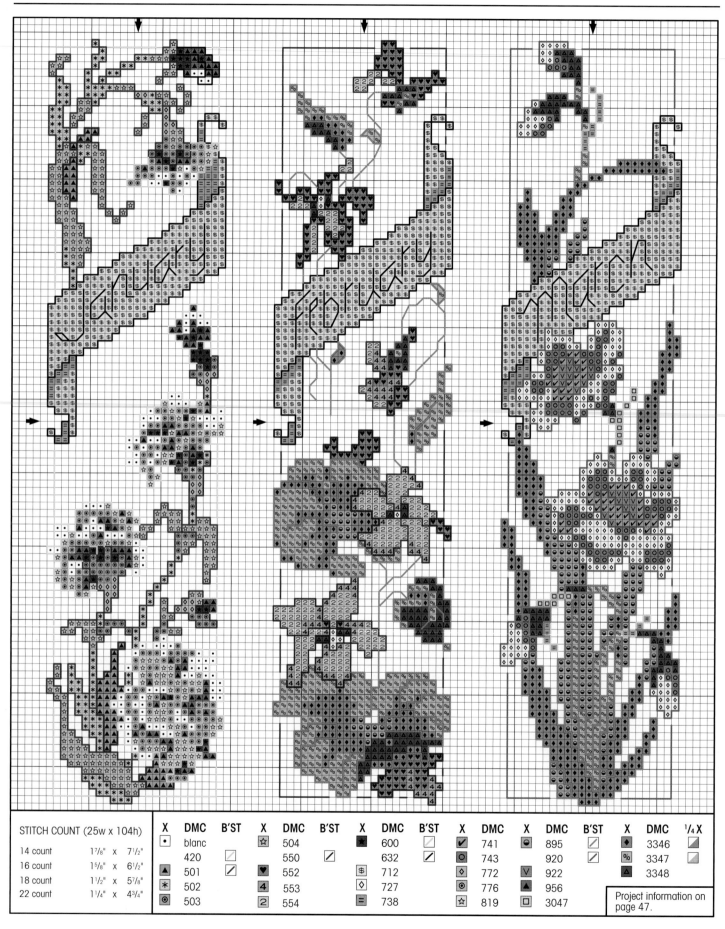

STITCH COUNT (25w x 104h)		X	DMC	B'ST	X	DMC	B'ST	X	DMC	B'ST	X	DMC	X	DMC	B'ST	X	DMC	¼X
		•	blanc		☆	504		★	600		✔	741	◒	895		◆	3346	
14 count	1⅞" x 7½"		420			550			632		◎	743		920		%	3347	
16 count	1⅝" x 6½"	▲	501		♥	552		$	712		◇	772	∨	922		△	3348	
18 count	1½" x 5⅞"	✳	502		4	553		◇	727		⊙	776	▲	956				
22 count	1¼" x 4¾"	◉	503		2	554		=	738		☆	819	▢	3047				

Project information on page 47.

X	DMC	B'ST	X	DMC	¼ X	B'ST	X	DMC	¼ X	B'ST	X	DMC	B'ST	X	DMC	B'ST	X	DMC	¼ X
•	blanc		△	352				632		◪		895	◪	✕	932		○	3347	◪
▲	304	◪	☆	353	◪		$	712	◪		＋	899		2	948		>	3348	
■	309		▲	561	◪	◪	=	738			⊖	910		☆	955		•	632 French Knot	
★	335		•	562	◪		−	772	◪		△	912		◇	3326				
	350	◪	4	563	◪	□	828				931	◪	▦	3345	◪			

45

BIRTHDAY BOUQUETS

X	DMC	B'ST		X	DMC	¼X	B'ST		X	DMC	¼X	B'ST		X	DMC		X	DMC	B'ST		X	DMC	B'ST
⬤	312	╱		‰	501		╱		▽	562	╱			$	712		4	754			8	3347	
△	341			★	502				⌀	564				=	738		-	772			◇	3348	
$	347	╱		⊙	503				▣	603				◆	743		✠	922			■	3350	╱
✳	350			+	504				○	604				U	744		V	963			☆	3756	
2	352			▲	561	◪	╱			632		╱		✕	746		⊠	3345	╱				

46

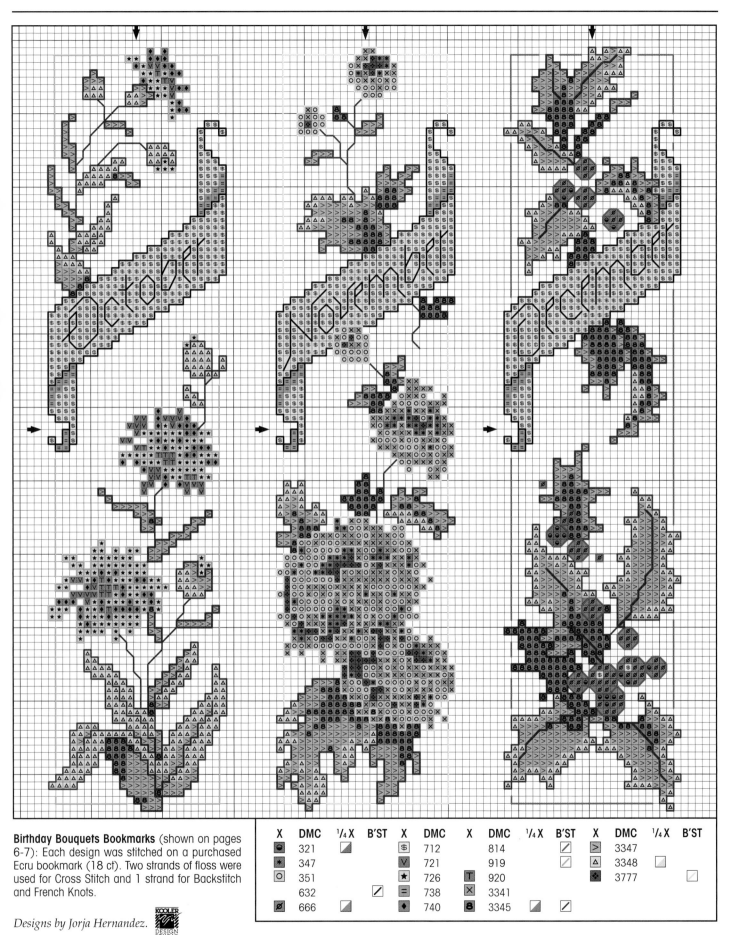

Birthday Bouquets Bookmarks (shown on pages 6-7): Each design was stitched on a purchased Ecru bookmark (18 ct). Two strands of floss were used for Cross Stitch and 1 strand for Backstitch and French Knots.

Designs by Jorja Hernandez.

X	DMC	¹/₄ X	B'ST	X	DMC	X	DMC	¹/₄ X	B'ST	X	DMC	¹/₄ X	B'ST
◕	321	◪		$	712		814		◿	>	3347		
✶	347			V	721		919		◿	△	3348	◳	
O	351			★	726	T	920			✹	3777		◿
	632		◿	=	738	X	3341						
ø	666	◪		◆	740	8	3345	◪	◿				

DEAREST BABY

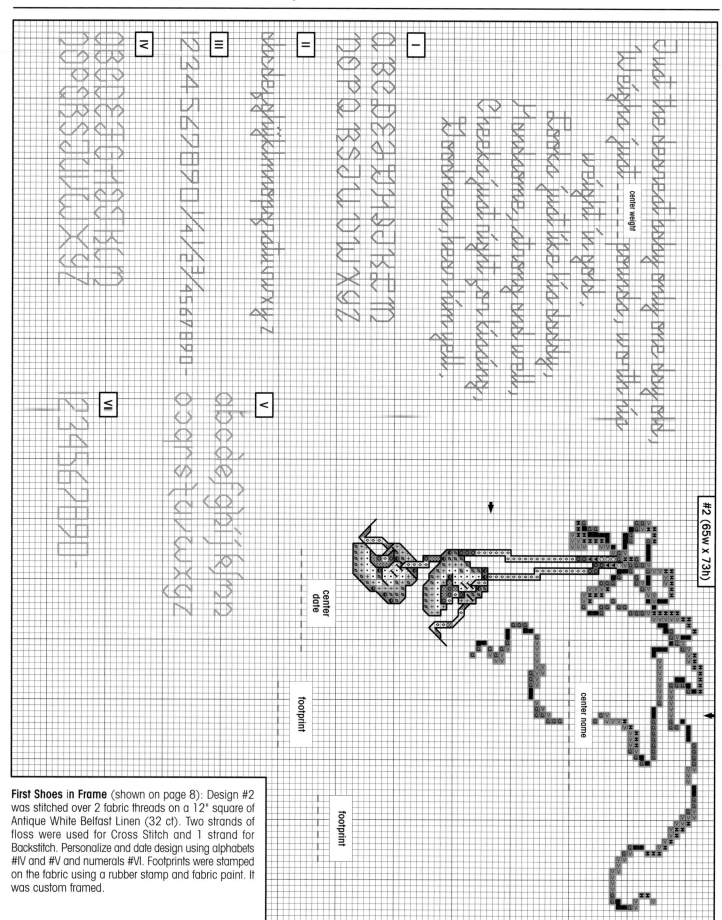

First Shoes in Frame (shown on page 8): Design #2 was stitched over 2 fabric threads on a 12" square of Antique White Belfast Linen (32 ct). Two strands of floss were used for Cross Stitch and 1 strand for Backstitch. Personalize and date design using alphabets #IV and #V and numerals #VI. Footprints were stamped on the fabric using a rubber stamp and fabric paint. It was custom framed.

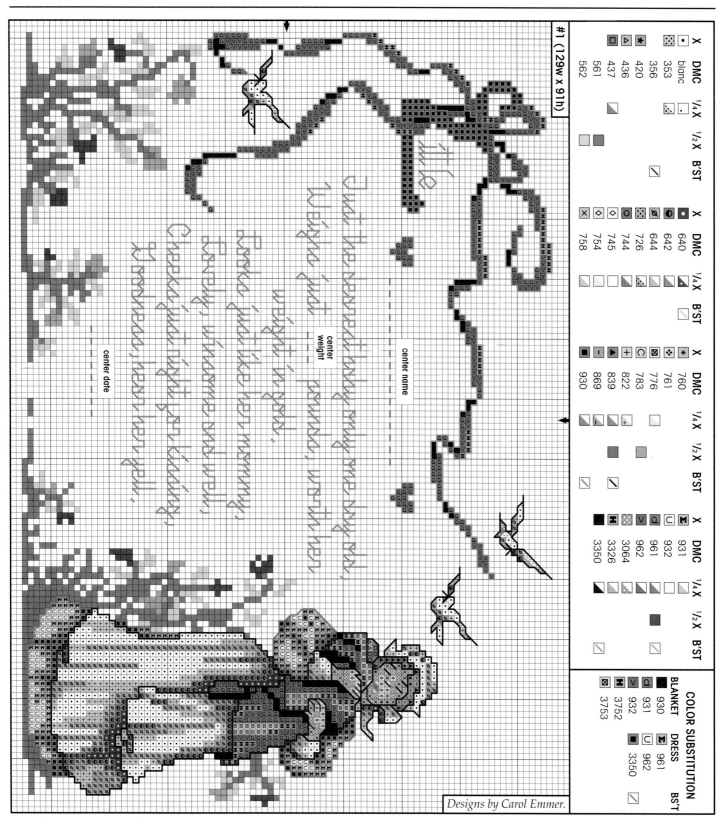

#1 (129w x 91h)

Designs by Carol Emmer.

X	1/4X	1/2X	B'ST	DMC
				blanc
				353
				356
				420
				436
				437
				561
				562

X	1/4X	B'ST	DMC
			640
			642
			644
			726
			744
			745
			754
			758

X	1/4X	1/2X	B'ST	DMC
				760
				761
				776
				783
				822
				839
				869
				930

X	1/4X	1/2X	B'ST	DMC
				931
				932
				961
				962
				3064
				3326
				3350

COLOR SUBSTITUTION

BLANKET: 930, 931, 932, 3752, 3753

DRESS: 961, 962, 3350

BS'T

center date
center name
center weight

Note: For each design, 2 strands of floss were used for Cross Stitch and 1 strand for Half Cross Stitch and Backstitch. Personalize and date designs using alphabets #I and #II and numerals #III. For a boy, use the Blanket and Dress Color Substitution list and the alternate verse.

Birth Sampler in Frame (shown on page 9): Design #1 was stitched over 2 fabric threads on a 16" x 14" piece of Antique White Belfast Linen (32 ct). It was custom framed.

Birth Sampler Pillow (shown on pages 8-9): Design #1 was stitched over 2 fabric threads on a 16" x 14" piece of Antique White Belfast Linen (32 ct). To complete pillow, see Finishing Instructions, page 82.

49

BLESSED WITH FRIENDS

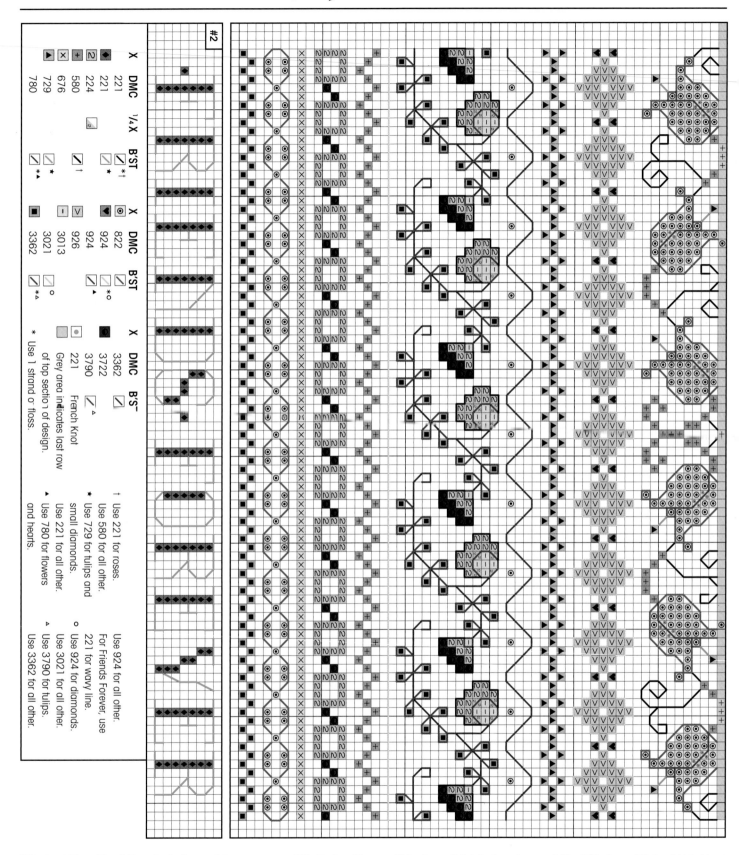

X	DMC	1/4 X	B'ST		X	DMC	B'ST		X	DMC	B'S
▶	221		▨	★†	■	822	▨	★○	□	3362	▨
✕	221		▨	★		924	▨	▶	■	3722	
+	224	▨	▨		◀	924				3790	▨ △
▨	580		▨	†	⊙	926					French Knot
◆	676		▨	★	I	221					Grey area indicates last row
	729		▨	★▶	V	3013					of top section of design.
	780			★▲		3021			○		Use 1 strand of floss.
					■	3362		△			

† Use 221 for roses.

★ Use 580 for all other. For Friends Forever, use

221 for wavy line.

○ Use 924 for diamonds,

small diamonds.

▶ Use 221 for all other.

★ Use 729 for tulips and

◆ Use 924 for all other.

Use 3021 for all other.

Use 3790 for tulips.

★ Use 780 for flowers

and hearts.

▲ Use 3362 for all other.

"The Lord Bless Thee" Sampler in Frame (shown on page 11): Design #1 was stitched over 2 fabric threads on a 14" x 18" piece of Natural Irish Linen (28 ct). Three strands of floss were used for Cross Stitch and 2 strands for Backstitch and French Knots, unless otherwise noted in the color key. It was custom framed.

Design by Kooler Design Studio.

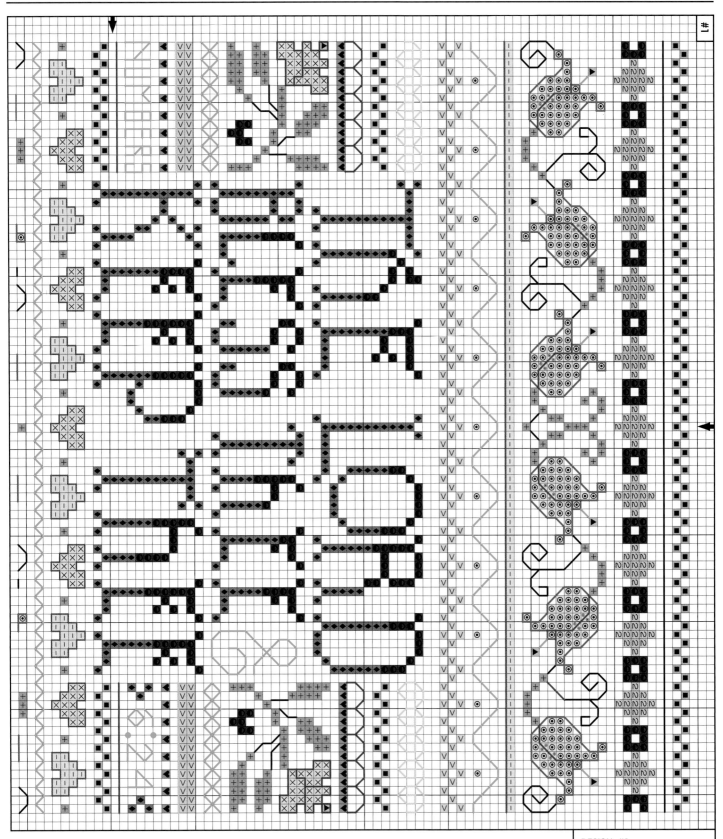

"Friends Forever " in Frame (shown on page 10): A portion of Design #1 (refer to photo), substituting Design #2 for the tulip and diamond rows, was stitched over 2 fabric threads on an 11" x 13" piece of Natural Irish Linen (28 ct). Three strands of floss were used for Cross Stitch and 2 strands for Backstitch, unless otherwise noted in the color key. It was custom framed.

DESIGN #1
STITCH COUNT (89w x 137h)

14 count	6³/₈"	x 9⁷/₈"
16 count	5⁵/₈"	x 8⁵/₈"
18 count	5"	x 7⁵/₈"
22 count	4¹/₈"	x 6¹/₄"

UNITED IN MATRIMONY

All project information on pages 54-56.

X	DMC	¼X	B'ST
•	blanc		
•	ecru	.	
	315		/
■*	315 & 3740·		
V*	316 & 3042	◪	
▣	422	◪	
II*	422 & 3045		
◇*	422 & 3046		
□	452		
◉*	452 & 3032	◪	
∧	453		
Σ*	453 & 3782		
■	500		
•*	500 & 520	◪	
▼	501		
✔	501 & 3362	◪	
▣'	502 & 522		

X	DMC	¼X	B'ST
△*	502 & 3363	◪	
✱*	503 & 523	◪	
◪*	504 & 524	◪	
✕	520		◪
–	522		
⍵	523		
8	524		
	640		◪
P	762		
∩	778 & 3747	◪	
	930		◪
◆*	930 & 3746		
□†	931		
☆*	931 & 340		
□†	932		
▽*	932 & 341		
	3032		◪*
▲*	3032 & 3045		◪

X	DMC	¼X	B'ST
=	3033		◪
O	3041		
⊠*	3041 & 3726		◪
<	3042		
✖	3045		
✤	3046		
♥	3362		
◓	3363		
∏	3743		
⊥*	3747 & 3752		
	3787		◪
∅*	501 & 3363	Lazy Daisy	
•	Mill Hill Bead - 03005		
•	Mill Hill Bead - 03021		
▨	Grey area indicates last row of previous section of design.		

DMC		SPECIALTY STITCH
ecru ▲	▥	Satin Stitch
422 & * 3033	✳	Upright Cross Stitch
422 & * 3033	⊠	Plaited Stitch
422 & * 3033	✺	Eight-Sided Eyelet
422 & * 3033	✲	Half Diamond Eyelet
778 & ° 3747	▥	Satin Stitch

DMC		SPECIALTY STITCH
3032 & ▲ 30543	/	Whipped Backstitch
3032 & □ 30712	/	Whipped Backstitch
3033 ★	▨	Plaited Cross Stitch
3033 ★	▩	Rhodes Stitch
3042 ★	/	Algerian Eye
3787 & ▲ 30712	/	Whipped Backstitch
30543 ■	▥	Satin Stitch
30712 ■	▥	Satin Stitch

* For linen, use 1 strand of each floss color listed. For Lugana, use 2 strands of first floss color listed and 1 strand of second floss color listed.

† Use 1 strand of floss for letters and numbers.

★ Use 2 strands of floss.

▲ Use 3 strands of floss.

° Use 2 strands of first floss color listed and 1 strand of second floss color listed.

▲ Use 2 strands of first floss color for Backstitch and 1 strand of Rayon floss color for whipping.

□ Use 1 strand of first floss color for Backstitch and 1 strand of Rayon floss color for whipping.

■ For linen, use 2 strands of Rayon floss. For Lugana, use 3 strands of Rayon floss.

STITCH COUNT (140w x 168h)		
14 count	10"	x 12"
16 count	8³/₄"	x 10¹/₂"
18 count	7⁷/₈"	x 9³/₈"
22 count	6³/₈"	x 7³/₄"

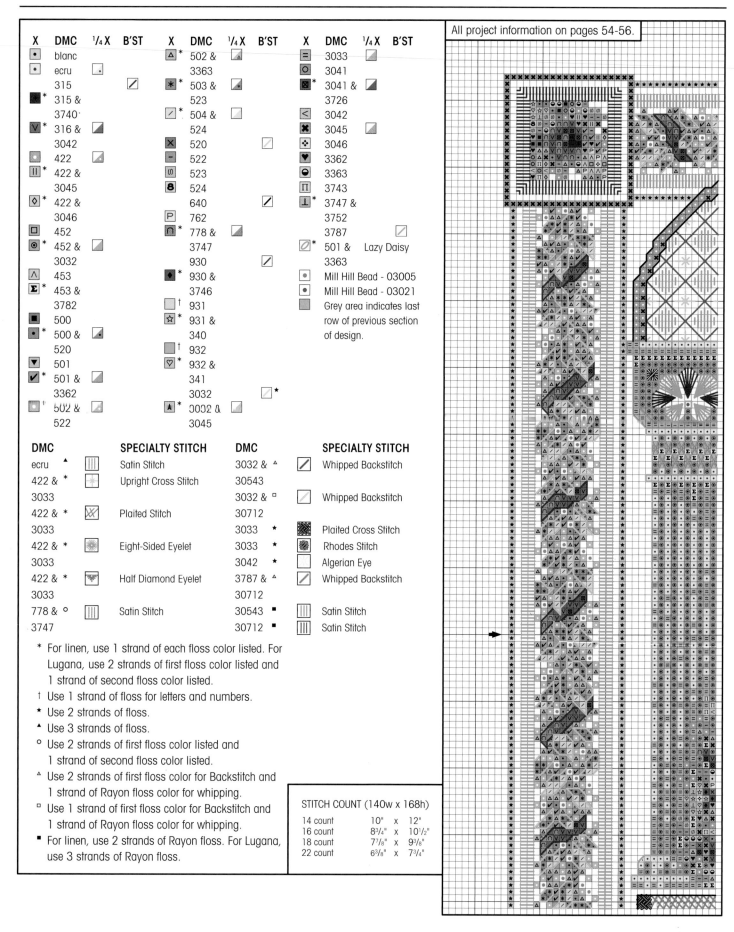

X	DMC	¼X	B'ST	X	DMC	¼X	B'ST	X	DMC	¼X	B'ST
•	blanc			△*	502 & 3363	◢		=	3033	◢	
•	ecru	◢		✳*	503 & 523	◢		O	3041		
	315		/	/*	504 & 524	◢		⊠	3041 & 3726	◢	
■*	315 & 3740			✕	520		/	<	3042		
V*	316 & 3042	◢		–	522			✕	3045		
•	422	◢		⦰	523			❖	3046		
II*	422 & 3045			8	524			♥	3362		
◇*	422 & 3046				640		/	◉	3363		
□	452			P	762			Π	3743		
◉*	452 & 3032	◢		∩*	778 & 3747		/	⊥*	3747 & 3752		
∧	453			◆*	930 & 3746				3787		/
Σ*	453 & 3782			□†	931			∅*	501 & 3363	Lazy Daisy	
■	500			☆*	931 & 340			•	Mill Hill Bead - 03005		
•*	500 & 520	◢		□†	932			•	Mill Hill Bead - 03021		
▼	501			▽*	932 & 341			▨	Grey area indicates last row of previous section of design.		
✓*	501 & 3362				3032		/*				
•*	502 & 522	◢		★*	3032 & 3045		/				

DMC		SPECIALTY STITCH	DMC		SPECIALTY STITCH
ecru ▲	▦	Satin Stitch	3032 & ▲ 30543	◢	Whipped Backstitch
422 & * 3033	✳	Upright Cross Stitch	3032 & □ 30712	◢	Whipped Backstitch
422 & * 3033	⊠	Plaited Stitch	3033 ★	▨	Plaited Cross Stitch
422 & * 3033	✺	Eight-Sided Eyelet	3033 ★	▨	Rhodes Stitch
422 & * 3033	✦	Half Diamond Eyelet	3042 ★		Algerian Eye
778 & ° 3747	▦	Satin Stitch	3787 & ▲ 30712	◢	Whipped Backstitch
			30543 ■	▦	Satin Stitch
			30712 ■	▦	Satin Stitch

* For linen, use 1 strand of each floss color listed. For Lugana, use 2 strands of first floss color listed and 1 strand of second floss color listed.

† Use 1 strand of floss for letters and numbers.

★ Use 2 strands of floss.

▲ Use 3 strands of floss.

° Use 2 strands of first floss color listed and 1 strand of second floss color listed.

△ Use 2 strands of first floss color for Backstitch and 1 strand of Rayon floss color for whipping.

□ Use 1 strand of first floss color for Backstitch and 1 strand of Rayon floss color for whipping.

■ For linen, use 2 strands of Rayon floss. For Lugana, use 3 strands of Rayon floss.

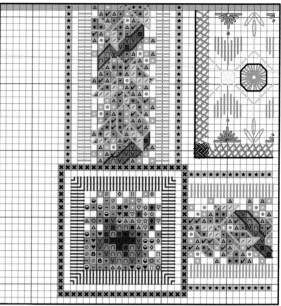

Wedding Sampler in Frame (shown on page 13): The design was stitched over 2 fabric threads on a 17" x 19" piece of Cream Belfast Linen (32 ct). Two strands of floss were used for Cross Stitch and Lazy Daisy Stitches and 1 strand for Backstitch, unless otherwise noted in the color key. Refer to chart for type of thread and number of strands used for Specialty Stitches. See Specialty Stitch Diagrams, pages 56 and 96. Attach beads using 1 strand of DMC ecru floss for cream beads and 1 strand of DMC 778 floss for rose beads. See Attaching Beads, page 95. Personalize and date design stitching over 1 fabric thread and using 1 strand of floss for Cross Stitch and Backstitch. Use alphabets and numerals #1 and #2 for names and #3, #4, and #5 for date. It was custom framed.

Wedding Sampler Pillow (shown on page 15): A portion of the design (refer to photo) was stitched over 2 fabric threads on a 14" x 13" piece of Cream Cashel Linen® (28 ct). Two strands of floss were used for Cross Stitch and 1 strand for Backstitch, unless otherwise noted in the color key. Refer to chart for type of thread and number of strands used for Specialty Stitches. See Specialty Stitch Diagrams, pages 56 and 96. Attach beads using 1 strand of DMC ecru floss. See Attaching Beads, page 95. Personalize and date design stitching over 1 fabric thread and using 1 strand of floss for Cross Stitch and Backstitch. Use alphabets and numerals #1 and #2 for names and #3, #4, and #5 for date.

For pillow, you will need a 7½" x 8½" piece of fabric for backing, 57" length of 2½"w pregathered lace, and polyester fiberfill.

Centering design, trim stitched piece to measure 7½" x 8½".

For lace ruffle, press short edges of lace ½" to wrong side. Matching raw edges of stitched piece and bound edge of lace, machine baste through all layers ½" from edges. Blind stitch pressed edges together.

Matching right sides and leaving an opening for turning, use a ½" seam allowance to sew stitched piece and backing fabric together. Trim seam allowances diagonally at corners; turn pillow right side out, carefully pushing corners outward. Stuff pillow with polyester fiberfill and blind stitch opening closed.

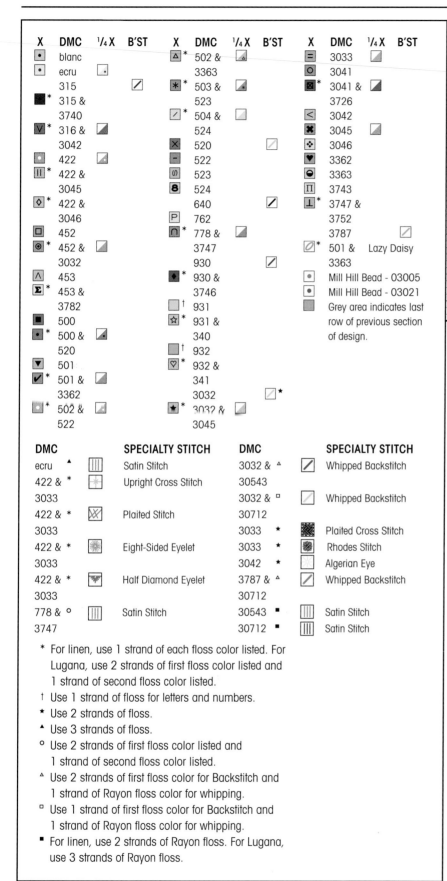

Heart Border Candle Band (shown on page 12): A portion of the design (refer to photo) was stitched over 2 fabric threads on a 17" x 6" piece of Cream Cashel Linen® (28 ct). Two strands of floss were used for Cross Stitch and Lazy Daisy Stitches and 1 strand for Backstitch, unless otherwise noted in the color key. Refer to chart for type of thread and number of strands used for Specialty Stitches. See Specialty Stitch Diagrams, pages 56 and 96. Attach beads using 1 strand of DMC 778 floss. See Attaching Beads, page 95.

Centering design, trim stitched piece to measure 15" x 4¹/₂".

Matching right sides and long edges, fold stitched piece in half. Using a ¹/₄" seam allowance, sew long edges together; trim seam allowance to ¹/₈" and turn stitched piece right side out. With seam centered in back, press stitched piece flat.

Wrap candle band around candle, turning raw edges to wrong side so that ends meet; blind stitch short ends together.

Anniversary Album (shown on page 14): A portion of the design (refer to photo) was stitched over 2 fabric threads on a 15" x 16" piece of Cream Lugana (25 ct). Three strands of floss were used for Cross Stitch and 1 strand for Backstitch, unless otherwise noted in the color key. Refer to chart for type of thread and number of strands used for Specialty Stitches. See Specialty Stitch Diagrams, pages 56 and 96. Attach beads using 1 strand of DMC ecru floss. See Attaching Beads, page 95. Personalize and date design stitching over 1 fabric thread and using 1 strand of floss for Cross Stitch and Backstitch. Use alphabets and numerals #1 and #2 for names and #3, #4, and #5 for date.

For album, you will need an 11" x 12" photo album with a 2¹/₂" spine, 1 yard of 44"w fabric, 24¹/₂" x 12" piece of batting for album, 8" x 9" piece of batting for stitched piece, two 10¹/₂" x 11¹/₂" pieces of poster board, tracing paper, pencil, 8" x 9" piece of adhesive mounting board, 31" length of ¹/₄" dia. purchased cord, and clear-drying craft glue.

Cut two 3" x 11¹/₂" strips of fabric. Glue one long edge of one strip ¹/₄" under one long side of metal spine inside album; glue remaining edges of strip to album. Repeat with remaining strip and long side of metal spine; allow to dry.

Continued on page 56.

UNITED IN MATRIMONY

Glue batting to outside of album. Cut a 26½" x 14" piece of fabric for outside of album. Center album, batting side down, on wrong side of fabric; fold fabric at corners to inside of album and glue in place. At center bottom of album, turn a 4" section of fabric ¼" to wrong side (**Fig. 1**); glue folded edge under spine of album. Repeat at center top of album. Fold remaining edges of fabric to inside of album and glue in place; allow to dry.

Fig. 1

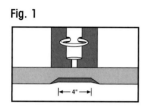

Cut two 12½" x 13½" pieces of fabric for inside covers. Center one piece of poster board on wrong side of one piece of fabric; fold edges of fabric to back of poster board and glue in place. Glue wrong side of covered poster board to inside of front cover of album

approximately ¼" from top, bottom, and outside edges of album. Repeat with remaining piece of fabric and poster board for inside back cover.

For pattern, fold tracing paper in half and place fold on dashed line of pattern; trace pattern onto tracing paper. Cut out pattern; unfold and press flat. Draw around pattern once on mounting board and once on batting; cut out. Remove paper from mounting board and press batting piece onto mounting board.

Referring to photo, position pattern on wrong side of stitched piece; pin pattern in place. Cut stitched piece **1" larger** than pattern on all sides. Clip ½" into edge of stitched piece at ½" intervals. Center wrong side of stitched piece over batting on mounting board piece; fold edges of stitched piece to back of mounting board and glue in place. Center and glue wrong side of mounted stitched piece to front cover.

Beginning at bottom center of stitched piece, glue cord around outside edge of stitched piece, overlapping ends of cord.

Floral Jar Lid (shown on page 15): A portion of the design (refer to photo) was stitched over 2 fabric threads on a 6" square of Cream Lugana (25 ct). Three strands of floss were used for Cross Stitch and Satin Stitch. See Specialty Stitch Diagrams, page 96. It was inserted in the lid of a round porcelain jar (2⅝" dia. opening).

SPECIALTY STITCH DIAGRAMS
(**Note:** Bring threaded needle up at 1 and all odd numbers and down at 2 and all even numbers.)

PULLED STITCHES
When working Pulled Stitches, fabric threads should be pulled tightly together to create an opening in the fabric around the stitch. Figs. show placement of stitch but do not show pulling of the fabric threads. Keep tension even throughout work.

Algerian Eye Stitch: An "eye" is formed in the center of this stitch. Come up at 1, go down in center, and pull tightly toward 3. Come up at 3, go down in center, and pull tightly toward 5; continue working in this manner until stitch is complete (stitches 5-15) (**Fig. 1**).

Fig. 1

Diamond Eyelet and Half Diamond Eyelet Stitches: An "eye" is formed in the center of this stitch. Come up at 1, go down in center, and pull tightly toward 3. Come up at 3, go down in center, and pull tightly toward 5; continue working in this manner until stitch is complete (stitches 5-31) as shown in **Fig. 2**. For **Half Diamond Eyelet** work stitches 1-17 in the same manner. The number of threads worked over will vary according to chart.

Fig. 2

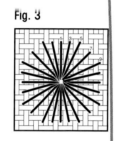

Eight-sided Eyelet Stitch: An "eye" is formed in the center of this stitch. Come up at 1, go down in center, and pull tightly toward 3. Come up at 3, go down in center, and pull tightly toward 5; continue working in this manner until stitch is complete as shown in **Fig. 3**.

Fig. 3

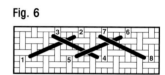

Four-sided Stitch: This continuous stitch is worked from left to right. Come up at 1 and pull tightly toward 2; then go down at 2 and pull tightly toward 1. Work stitches 3-14 in same manner (**Fig. 4**). Continue working in the same manner to end of row.

Fig. 4

EMBROIDERY STITCHES

Upright Cross Stitch: This decorative stitch is formed by working four stitches. Work Upright Cross Stitch (stitches 1-4) first, then work Cross Stitch (stitches 5-8) over center of Upright Cross Stitch as shown in **Fig. 5**. The top stitch of the Upright Cross must be made in the same direction on all stitches worked.

Fig. 5

Herringbone Stitch: This overlapping stitch is worked continuously from left to right. The number of threads worked over will vary according to chart. Complete first stitch (stitches 1-4); then work next stitch (stitches 5-8) as shown in **Fig. 6**. Work all consecutive stitches in the same manner as stitches 5-8.

Fig. 6

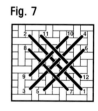

Plaited Cross Stitch: This decorative stitch is formed by working six stitches (stitches 1-12) as shown in **Fig. 7**.

Fig. 7

Plaited Stitch: This overlapping stitch is worked continuously from left to right. Complete first stitch (stitches 1-4); then work next stitch (stitches 5-8) as shown in **Fig. 8**. Work all consecutive stitches in the same manner as stitches 5-8.

Fig. 8

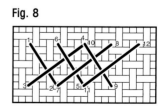

Continued on page 96.

56

SWEET HOLIDAY GREETINGS

X	DMC	B'ST	X	DMC
◆	347	✓	✦	3328
=	522		◉	3363
■	642		▽	3364
✕	760		•	Mill Hill Bead - 03021
‖	761			

STITCH COUNT (64w x 75h)

14 count	4⅝"	x	5⅜"
16 count	4"	x	4¾"
18 count	3⅝"	x	4¼"
22 count	3"	x	3½"

Millennium Sampler in Frame (shown on page 16): The design was stitched over 2 fabric threads on a 12" x 13" piece of Cream Belfast Linen (32 ct). Two strands of floss were used for Cross Stitch and 1 strand for Backstitch. Attach beads using 1 strand of DMC 822 floss. See Attaching Beads, page 95. It was custom framed.

Design by Linda Culp Calhoun.

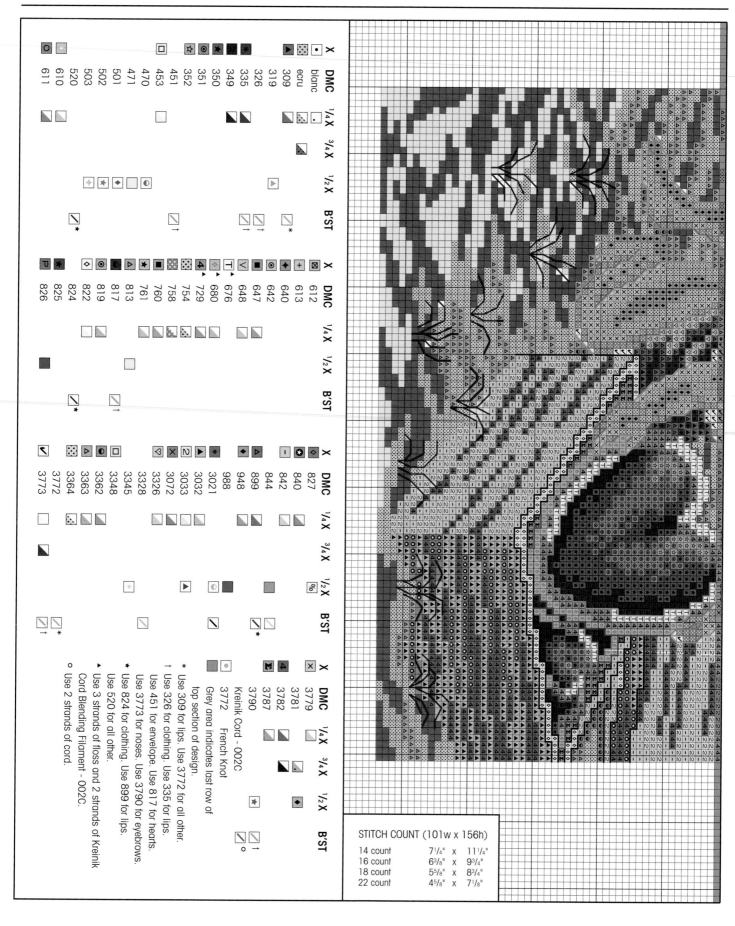

X	DMC	1/4 X	3/4 X	1/2 X	B'ST
	blanc				
	ecru				
	309				
	319				
	326				
	335				
	349				
	350				
	351				
	352				
	453				
	451				
	470				
	471				
	501				
	502				
	503				
	520				
	610				
	611				

X	DMC	1/4 X	1/2 X	B'ST
	612			
	613			
	640			
	642			
	647			
	648			
	676			
	680			
	729			
	754			
	758			
	760			
	761			
	813			
	817			
	819			
	822			
	824			
	825			
	826			

X	DMC	1/4 X	3/4 X	1/2 X	B'ST
	827				
	840				
	842				
	844				
	899				
	948				
	988				
	3021				
	3032				
	3033				
	3072				
	3326				
	3328				
	3345				
	3348				
	3362				
	3363				
	3364				
	3772				
	3773				

X	DMC	1/4 X	3/4 X	1/2 X	B'ST
	3779				
	3781				
	3782				
	3787				
	3790				
	3772 French Knot				
	Kreinik Cord - 002C				

Grey area indicates last row of top section of design.

* Use 309 for lips. Use 3772 for all other.
† Use 326 for clothing. Use 335 for lips.
Use 451 for envelope. Use 817 for hearts.
Use 3773 for noses. Use 3790 for eyebrows.
Use 824 for clothing. Use 899 for lips.
★ Use 520 for all other.
▲ Use 3 strands of floss and 2 strands of Kreinik Cord Blending Filament - 002C.
○ Use 2 strands of cord.

STITCH COUNT (101w x 156h)		
14 count	7 1/4" x	11 1/4"
16 count	6 3/8" x	9 3/4"
18 count	5 5/8" x	8 3/4"
22 count	4 5/8" x	7 1/8"

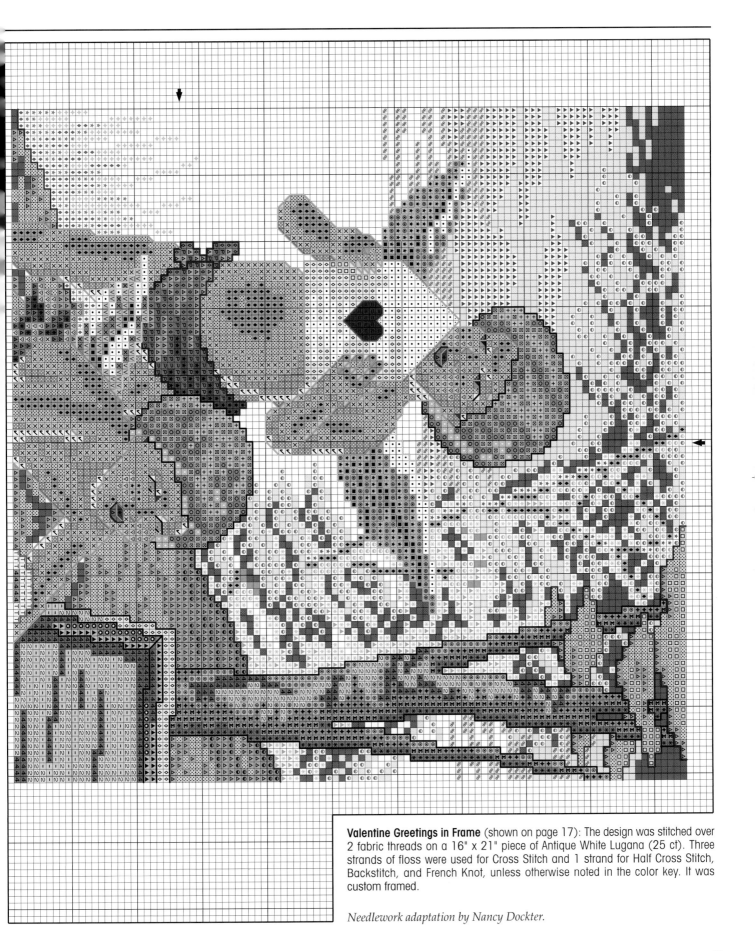

Valentine Greetings in Frame (shown on page 17): The design was stitched over 2 fabric threads on a 16" x 21" piece of Antique White Lugana (25 ct). Three strands of floss were used for Cross Stitch and 1 strand for Half Cross Stitch, Backstitch, and French Knot, unless otherwise noted in the color key. It was custom framed.

Needlework adaptation by Nancy Dockter.

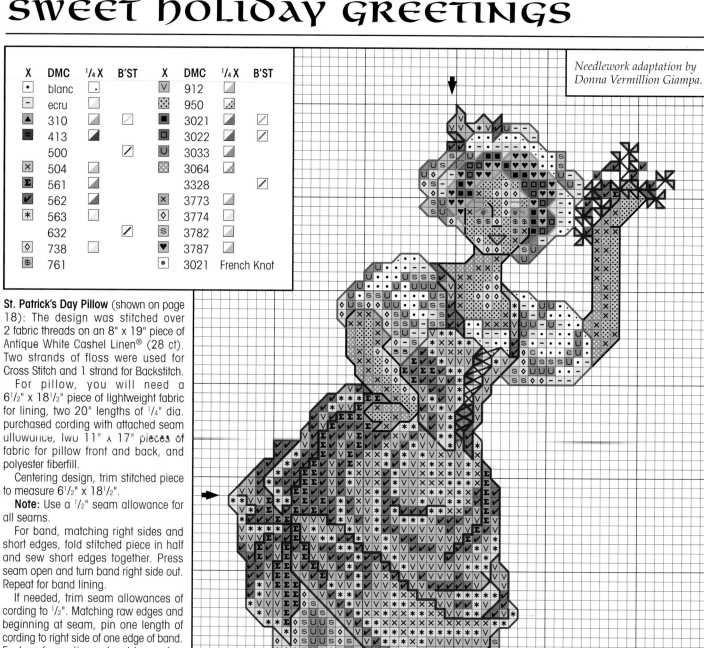

X	DMC	¼X	B'ST	X	DMC	¼X	B'ST
•	blanc	◩		V	912	◩	
−	ecru	◩		⁘	950	◩	
▲	310	◩	╱	■	3021	◩	╱
≡	413	◩		□	3022	◩	╱
	500		╱	U	3033	◩	
×	504	◩		⁘	3064	◩	
Σ	561	◩			3328		╱
✔	562	◩		×	3773	◩	
*	563	◩		◊	3774	◩	
	632		╱	S	3782	◩	
◊	738	◩		♥	3787	◩	
$	761			•	3021	French Knot	

Needlework adaptation by Donna Vermillion Giampa.

St. Patrick's Day Pillow (shown on page 18): The design was stitched over 2 fabric threads on an 8" x 19" piece of Antique White Cashel Linen® (28 ct). Two strands of floss were used for Cross Stitch and 1 strand for Backstitch.

For pillow, you will need a 6½" x 18½" piece of lightweight fabric for lining, two 20" lengths of ¼" dia. purchased cording with attached seam allowance, two 11" x 17" pieces of fabric for pillow front and back, and polyester fiberfill.

Centering design, trim stitched piece to measure 6½" x 18½".

Note: Use a ½" seam allowance for all seams.

For band, matching right sides and short edges, fold stitched piece in half and sew short edges together. Press seam open and turn band right side out. Repeat for band lining.

If needed, trim seam allowances of cording to ½". Matching raw edges and beginning at seam, pin one length of cording to right side of one edge of band. Ends of cording should overlap approximately 1½". Turn overlapped ends of cording toward outside edge of band; baste cording to band. Repeat for remaining length of cording and edge of band. Matching right sides and seam, and leaving an opening for turning, sew band and lining together. Turn band right side out and blind stitch opening closed.

For pillow, match right sides and raw edges of pillow front and back. Leaving an opening for turning, use a ½" seam allowance to sew fabric pieces together; trim seam allowances diagonally at corners. Turn pillow right side out, carefully pushing corners outward; stuff pillow lightly with polyester fiberfill and blind stitch opening closed.

Referring to photo, place band around pillow.

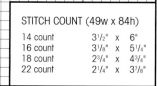

STITCH COUNT (49w x 84h)

14 count	3½"	x	6"
16 count	3⅛"	x	5¼"
18 count	2¾"	x	4¾"
22 count	2¼"	x	3⅞"

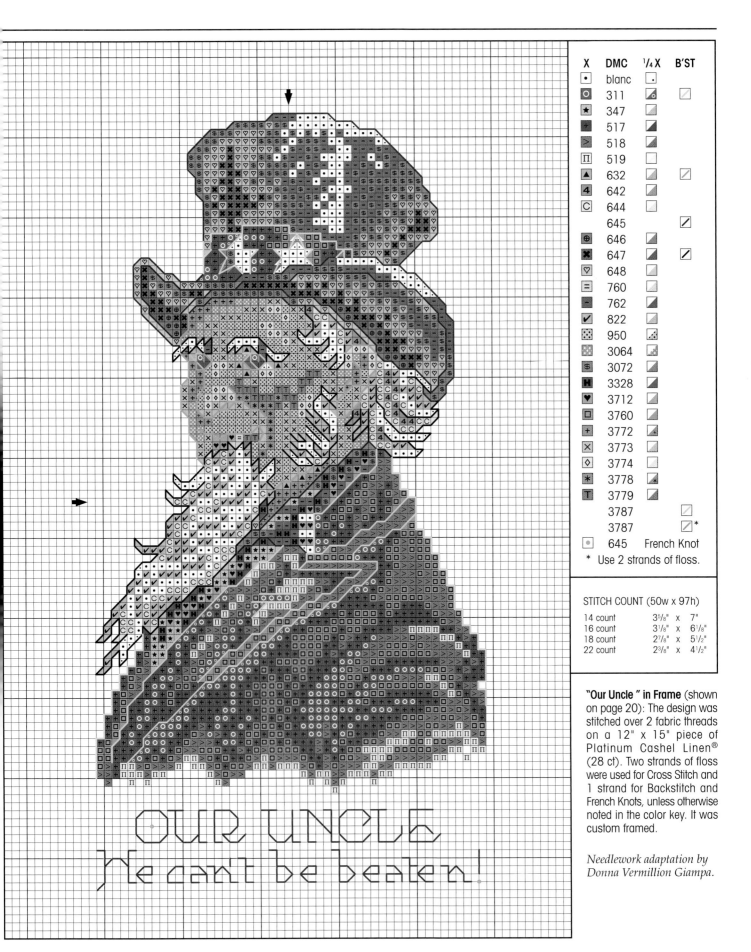

X	DMC	¼ X	B'ST
•	blanc	•	
○	311		
★	347		
+	517		
>	518		
⊓	519		
▲	632		
4	642		
C	644		
	645		
⊕	646		
✕	647		
♡	648		
=	760		
-	762		
✔	822		
⠿	950		
▨	3064		
$	3072		
H	3328		
♥	3712		
□	3760		
+	3772		
✕	3773		
◇	3774		
✳	3778		
T	3779		
	3787		
	3787		*
⊙	645	French Knot	

* Use 2 strands of floss.

STITCH COUNT (50w x 97h)

14 count	3⁵/₈"	x	7"
16 count	3¹/₈"	x	6¹/₈"
18 count	2⁷/₈"	x	5¹/₂"
22 count	2³/₈"	x	4¹/₂"

"Our Uncle" in Frame (shown on page 20): The design was stitched over 2 fabric threads on a 12" x 15" piece of Platinum Cashel Linen® (28 ct). Two strands of floss were used for Cross Stitch and 1 strand for Backstitch and French Knots, unless otherwise noted in the color key. It was custom framed.

Needlework adaptation by Donna Vermillion Giampa.

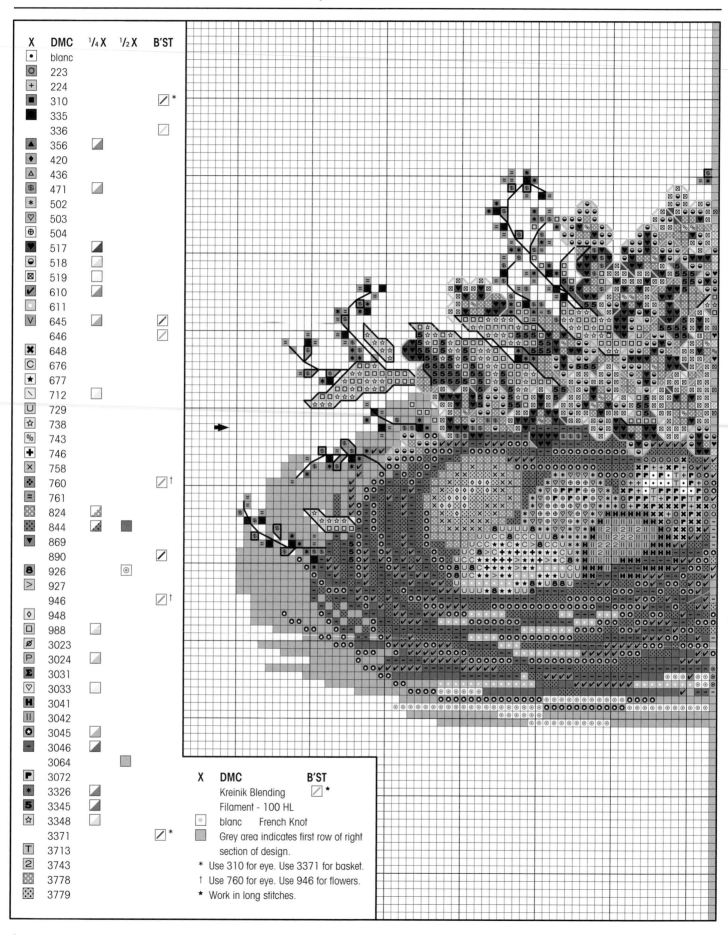

X	DMC	¼ X	½ X	B'ST
•	blanc			
◎	223			
+	224			
■	310			╱ *
◼	335			
	336			╱
▲	356	◣		
◆	420			
△	436			
$	471	◣		
*	502			
▽	503			
⊕	504			
▼	517	◣		
⊖	518	◣		
⊠	519	◻		
✔	610	◻		
▨	611			
V	645	◣		╱
	646	◻		╱
✖	648			
C	676			
★	677			
◺	712	◣		
U	729			
☆	738			
%	743			
✚	746			
✗	758			
❖	760			╱ †
=	761			
▨	824	◢		
▨	844	◢	◼	
▼	869			
	890			╱
8	926		◉	
>	927			
	946			╱ †
◇	948			
◻	988	◣		
∅	3023			
P	3024	◣		
Σ	3031			
▽	3033	◻		
H	3041			
‖	3042			
✿	3045	◣		
-	3046	◣		
	3064		◻	
▣	3072			
*	3326	◣		
5	3345	◣		
☆	3348	◻		
	3371			╱ *
T	3713			
2	3743			
▨	3778			
▨	3779			

X	DMC		B'ST
	Kreinik Blending Filament - 100 HL		╱ *
◦	blanc	French Knot	

Grey area indicates first row of right section of design.

* Use 310 for eye. Use 3371 for basket.

† Use 760 for eye. Use 946 for flowers.

★ Work in long stitches.

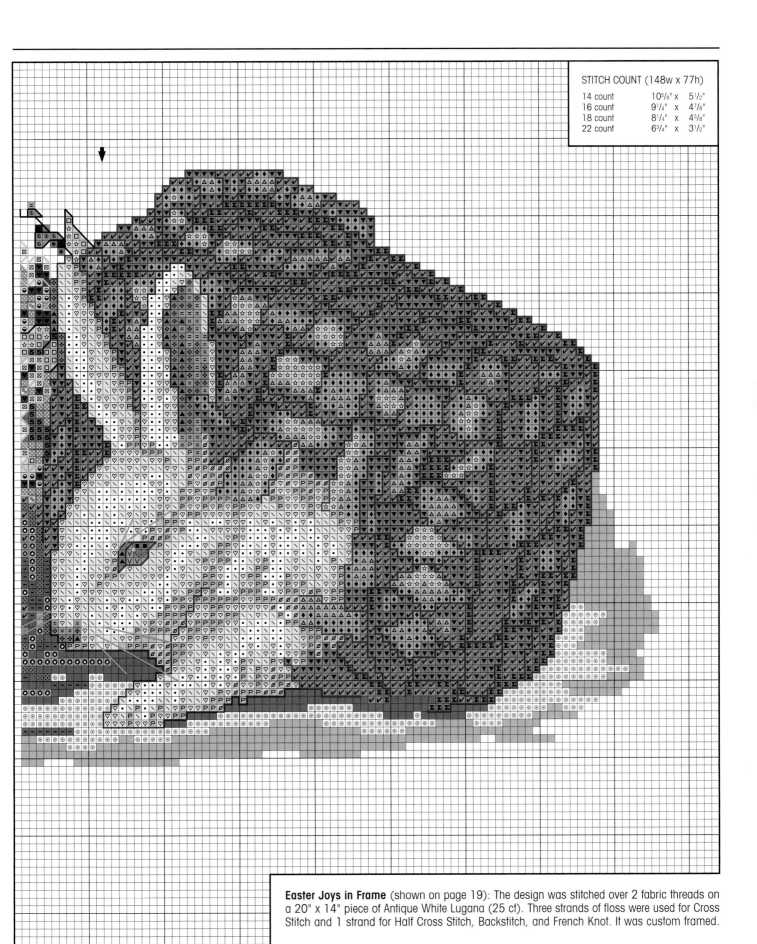

STITCH COUNT (148w x 77h)

14 count	10⁵/₈" x	5¹/₂"
16 count	9¹/₄" x	4⁷/₈"
18 count	8¹/₄" x	4³/₈"
22 count	6³/₄" x	3¹/₂"

Easter Joys in Frame (shown on page 19): The design was stitched over 2 fabric threads on a 20" x 14" piece of Antique White Lugana (25 ct). Three strands of floss were used for Cross Stitch and 1 strand for Half Cross Stitch, Backstitch, and French Knot. It was custom framed.

Needlework adaptation by Jane Chandler.

SWEET HOLIDAY GREETINGS

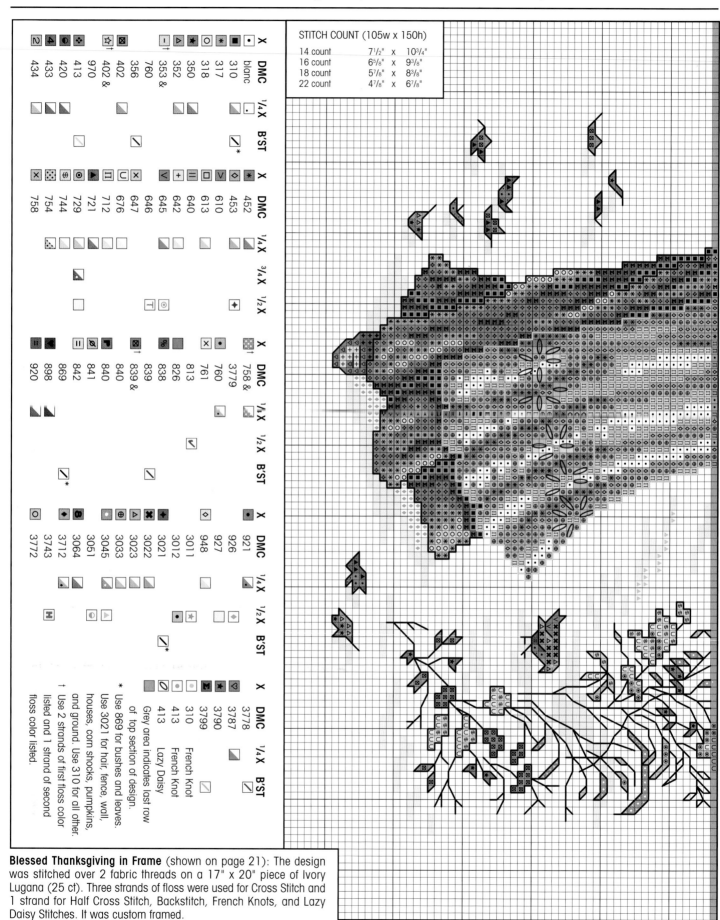

STITCH COUNT (105w x 150h)

count	width	height
14 count	7½"	x 10¾"
16 count	6⅝"	x 9⅜"
18 count	5⅞"	x 8⅜"
22 count	4⅞"	x 6⅞"

Color key (DMC), by section — column types: X, ¼X, ¾X, ½X, B'ST

Section 1 — DMC: blanc, 310, 317, 318, 350, 352, 353 &, 970, 402 &, 413, 420, 433, 434

Section 2 — DMC: 452, 453, 758 &, 3779, 760, 610, 613, 640, 642, 645, 646, 647, 676, 712, 721, 729, 744, 754, 758

Section 3 — DMC: 921, 926, 927, 948, 761, 813, 826, 838, 839, 839 &, 840, 840, 841, 842, 869, 898, 920

Section 4 — DMC: 3778, 3787, 3790, 3799, 3772, 3743, 3712, 3064, 3051, 3045, 3033, 3023, 3022, 3021, 3012, 3011

310 — French Knot
413 — French Knot
413 — Lazy Daisy

* Grey area indicates last row of top section of design.

Use 869 for bushes and leaves. Use 3021 for hair, fence, wall, houses, corn shocks, pumpkins, and ground. Use 310 for all other.

† Use 2 strands of first floss color listed and 1 strand of second floss color listed.

Blessed Thanksgiving in Frame (shown on page 21): The design was stitched over 2 fabric threads on a 17" x 20" piece of Ivory Lugana (25 ct). Three strands of floss were used for Cross Stitch and 1 strand for Half Cross Stitch, Backstitch, French Knots, and Lazy Daisy Stitches. It was custom framed.

Needlework adaptation by Nancy Dockter.

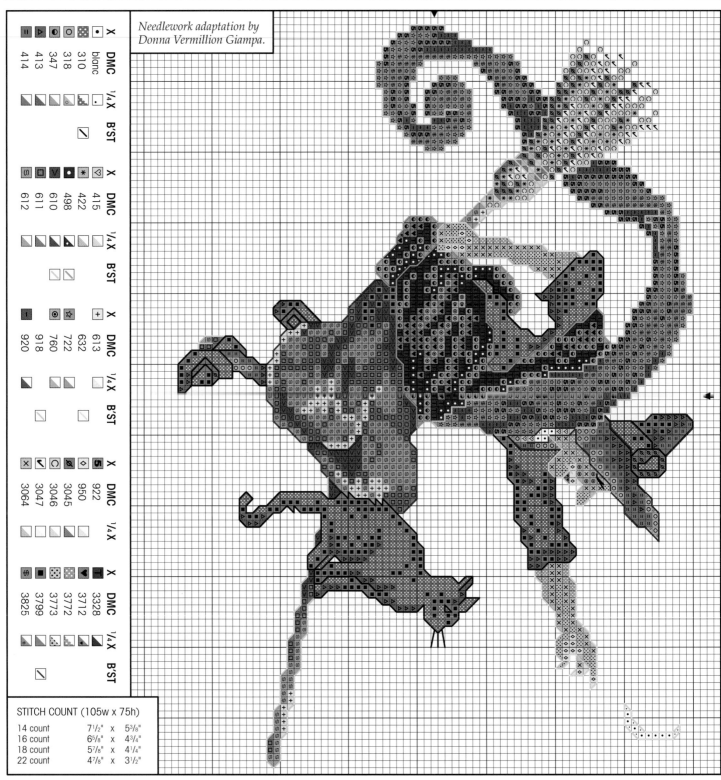

Needlework adaptation by Donna Vermillion Giampa.

					X
					DMC
414	413	347	318	310	blanc
					¼X
					B'ST

					X
					DMC
612	611	610	498	422	415
					¼X
					B'ST

					X
					DMC
920	918	760	722	632	613
					¼X
					B'ST

					X
					DMC
3064	3047	3046	3045	950	922
					¼X

					X
					DMC
3825	3799	3773	3772	3712	3328
					¼X
					B'ST

STITCH COUNT (105w x 75h)

14 count	7½"	x	5⅜"
16 count	6⅝"	x	4¾"
18 count	5⅞"	x	4¼"
22 count	4⅞"	x	3½"

Witch in Flight Wreath (shown on page 20): The design was stitched over 2 fabric threads on a 15" x 13" piece of Raw Belfast Linen (32 ct). Two strands of floss were used for Cross Stitch and 1 strand for Backstitch. We replaced moon with a purchased charm.

For pillow, you will need a 9" x 6¾" piece of Raw Belfast Linen for backing, 32" length of ¼" dia. purchased cording with attached seam allowance, and polyester fiberfill.

Centering design, trim stitched piece to measure 9" x 6¾".

If needed, trim seam allowances of cording to ½". Matching raw edges, pin cording to right side of stitched piece, making a ⅜" clip in seam allowance of cording at corners. Ends of cording should overlap approximately 4". Turn overlapped ends of cording toward outside edge of stitched piece; baste cording to stitched piece.

Matching right sides and raw edges, pin stitched piece and backing fabric together. Leaving an opening for turning, use a ½" seam allowance to sew pillow front and backing fabric together. Trim seam allowances diagonally at corners; turn pillow right side out, carefully pushing corners outward. Stuff pillow with polyester fiberfill and blind stitch opening closed. Attach pillow to a decorated 18" dia. grapevine wreath.

CHRISTMAS OFFERINGS

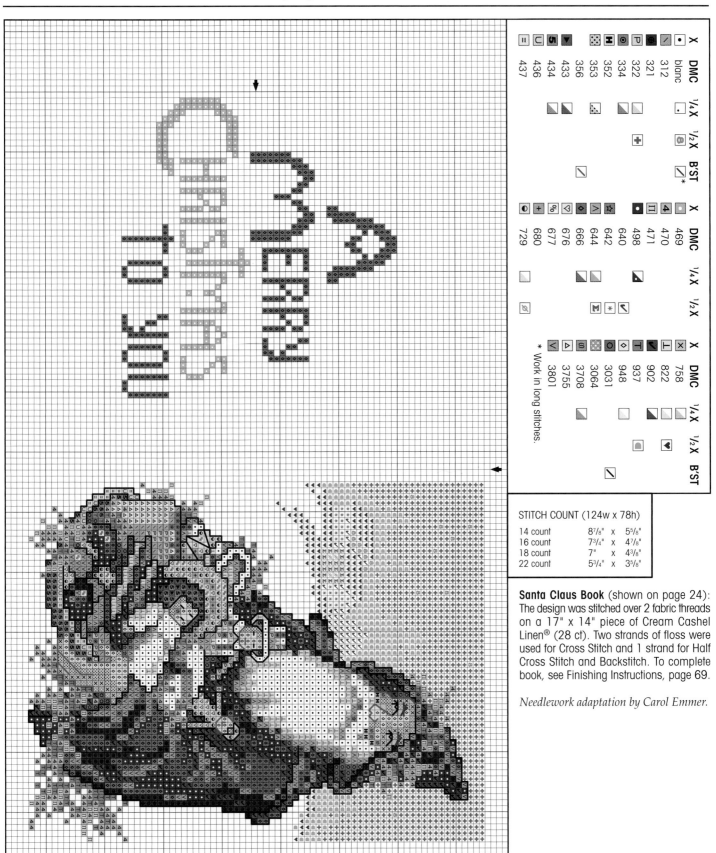

X	DMC	¼X	½X	B'ST
	437			
	436			
	434			
	433			
	356			
	353			
	352			
	334			
	322			
	321			
	312			
	blanc			

X	DMC	¼X	½X
	729		
	680		
	677		
	676		
	666		
	644		
	642		
	640		
	498		
	471		
	470		
	469		

X	DMC	¼X	½X	B'ST
	3801			
	3755			
	3708			
	3064			
	3031			
	948			
	937			
	902			
	822			
	758			

* Work in long stitches.

STITCH COUNT (124w x 78h)

14 count	8⅞"	x 5⅝"
16 count	7¾"	x 4⅞"
18 count	7"	x 4⅜"
22 count	5¾"	x 3⅝"

Santa Claus Book (shown on page 24): The design was stitched over 2 fabric threads on a 17" x 14" piece of Cream Cashel Linen® (28 ct). Two strands of floss were used for Cross Stitch and 1 strand for Half Cross Stitch and Backstitch. To complete book, see Finishing Instructions, page 69.

Needlework adaptation by Carol Emmer.

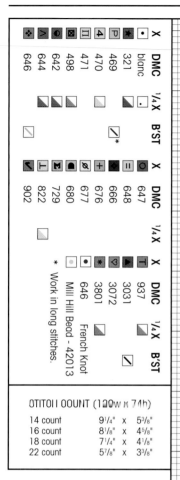

X	DMC	1/4X	B'ST
•	blanc	•	
★	321	◣	
P	469		⟋*
4	470	◣	
Π	471		
⊠	498	◣	
◐	642	◣	
>	644	◣	
✣	646		⟋
O	647		
=	648		
◆	666		
+	676		
⊘	677		
●	680		
M	729		
T	822	◣	
◥	902		
T	937	◣	
▶	3031		⟋
♡	3072		
✱	3801	◣	
•	646 French Knot		
●	Mill Hill Bead - 42013		

* Work in long stitches.

STITCH COUNT (129w x 74h)

14 count	9 1/4"	x	5 3/8"
16 count	8 1/8"	x	4 5/8"
18 count	7 1/4"	x	4 1/8"
22 count	5 7/8"	x	3 3/8"

Holiday Bells Book (shown on page 25): The design was stitched over 2 fabric threads on a 17" x 14" piece of Cream Cashel Linen® (28 ct). Two strands of floss were used for Cross Stitch and 1 strand for Backstitch and French Knots. Attach beads using 1 strand of DMC 321 floss. See Attaching Beads, page 95. To complete book, see Finishing Instructions, page 69.

Needlework adaptation by Carol Emmer.

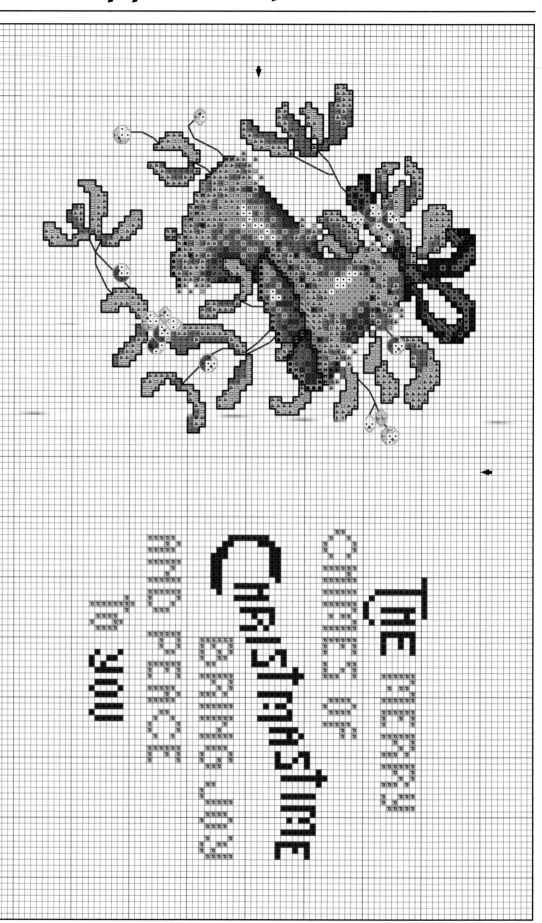

STITCH COUNT (132w x 81h)

14 count	9½"	x	5⅞"	
16 count	8¼"	x	5⅛"	
18 count	7⅜"	x	4½"	
22 count	6"	x	3¾"	

												DMC	B'ST
											X		
												321	
												469	
												470	
												471	
												498	
												666	
												676	
												902	
												937	
												3031	
												3801	

"Christmas Joys" Book (shown on pages 24-25): The design was stitched over 2 fabric threads on a 17" x 14" piece of Cream Cashel Linen® (28 ct). Two strands of floss were used for Cross Stitch and 1 strand for Backstitch.

Needlework adaptation by Carol Emmer.

FINISHING INSTRUCTIONS

Santa Claus, Holiday Bells, and "Christmas Joys" Books (shown on pages 24-25, charts on pages 67-69). For each book, you will need an 11" x 8" piece of fabric for backing, four 4¾" x 6¾" pieces of adhesive mounting board, four 4¾" x 6¾" pieces of batting, 36" length of ¼" dia. purchased cording with attached seam allowance, 10½" length of ⅜"w ribbon, clear-drying craft glue, and assorted charms.

Centering design, trim stitched piece to measure 11" x 8".

Remove paper from one mounting board piece and press one batting piece onto mounting board. Repeat with remaining mounting board pieces and batting.

Clip ½" into edge of stitched piece at ½" intervals. Center wrong side of left half of stitched piece over batting on one mounting board piece; repeat for right half of stitched piece, allowing a ½" space between mounting board pieces (**Fig. 1**). Fold edges of stitched piece to back of mounting boards and glue in place. For book back, repeat with backing fabric and remaining mounting board pieces.

Fig. 1

Beginning and ending at bottom center of stitched piece, glue cording seam allowance to wrong side of book front, overlapping ends of cording. Matching wrong sides and aligning mounting board pieces, glue book front and back together. Machine stitch book through all layers at center space between mounting board pieces. Referring to photo, glue one end of ribbon to back of book at center seam. Position ribbon over center seam on book front; trim end as desired. Referring to photo for placement, attach charms to book.

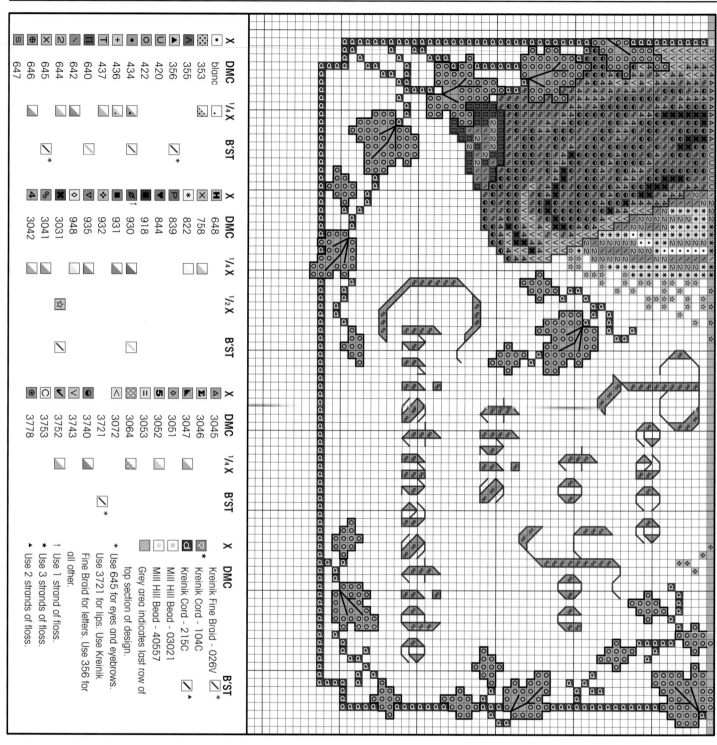

Color Key

X	DMC	1/4 X	B'ST
	blanc		
⊕	353		
×	355		
2	356		
/	420		
⬛	422		
T	434		
+	436		
•	437		
O	640		
▶	642		
▲	644		
	645		*
	646		
	647		

X	DMC	1/4 X	1/2 X	B'ST
4	648			
‰	758			
✕	822			
◇	839			
▽	844			
❖	918			
■	930			
∅	931			
■	932			
◀	935			
P	948			
*	3031			
X	3041			
H	3042			

X	DMC	1/4 X	B'ST
⊙	3045		
⊂	3046		
◤	3047		
∨	3051		
◐	3052		
∧	3053		
⋰	3064		
‖	3072		
5	3721		*
◇	3740		
◤	3743		
M	3752		
▷	3753		
	3778		

	DMC	X	B'ST
	Kreinik Fine Braid - 026V		*
	Kreinik Cord - 104C		
	Kreinik Cord - 215C		
	Mill Hill Bead - 03021		
	Mill Hill Bead - 40557		▶

Grey area indicates last row of top section of design.

* Use 645 for eyes and eyebrows. Use 3721 for lips. Use Kreinik Fine Braid for letters. Use 356 for all other.

† Use 1 strand of floss.
★ Use 3 strands of floss.
▶ Use 2 strands of floss.

Nativity in Frame (shown on page 23): The design was stitched over 2 fabric threads on a 14" x 18" piece of Raw Cashel Linen® (28 ct). Two strands of floss were used for Cross Stitch and 1 strand for Half Cross Stitch and Backstitch, unless otherwise noted in the color key. Attach beads using 1 strand of DMC blanc floss for cream bead and 1 strand of DMC 930 floss for gold beads. See Attaching Beads, page 95. It was custom framed.

Nativity Ornament (shown on page 22): A portion of the design (refer to photo) was stitched over 2 fabric threads on a 7" square of Raw Cashel Linen® (28 ct). Two strands of floss were used for Cross Stitch and 1 strand for Backstitch. Attach beads using 1 strand of DMC blanc floss for cream bead and 1 strand of DMC 930 floss for gold beads. See Attaching Beads, page 95.

For ornament, you will need a 7" square of Raw Cashel Linen® for backing, 5" x 7" piece of adhesive mounting board, 5" x 7" piece of batting, tracing paper, pencil, 13" length of ³⁄₈" dia. purchased cording with attached seam allowance, and clear-drying craft glue.

For pattern, fold tracing paper in half and place fold on dashed line of pattern; trace pattern onto tracing paper. Cut out pattern; unfold and press flat. Draw around pattern twice on mounting board and twice on batting; cut out. Remove paper from one mounting board piece and press one batting piece onto mounting board. Repeat with remaining mounting board and batting.

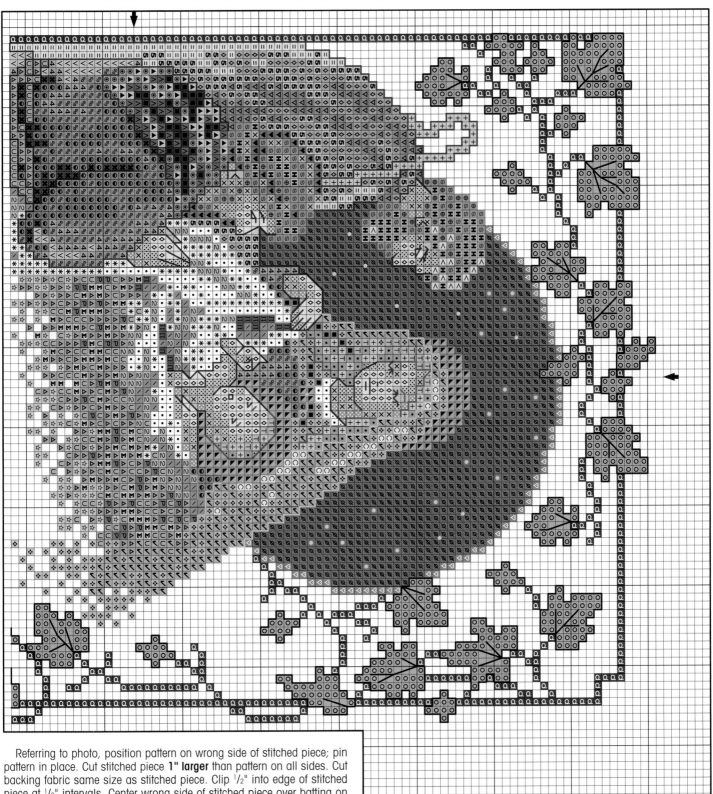

Referring to photo, position pattern on wrong side of stitched piece; pin pattern in place. Cut stitched piece **1" larger** than pattern on all sides. Cut backing fabric same size as stitched piece. Clip ¹/₂" into edge of stitched piece at ¹/₂" intervals. Center wrong side of stitched piece over batting on mounting board piece; fold edges of stitched piece to back of mounting board and glue in place. For ornament back, repeat with backing fabric and remaining mounting board.

Beginning and ending at bottom center of stitched piece, glue cording seam allowance to wrong side of ornament front, overlapping ends of cording. Matching wrong sides, glue ornament front and back together.

Needlework adaptation by Carol Emmer.

STITCH COUNT (86w x 134h)

14 count	6¹/₄"	x	9⁵/₈"
16 count	5³/₈"	x	8³/₈"
18 count	4⁷/₈"	x	7¹/₂"
22 count	4"	x	6¹/₈"

94w x 101h

"I See the Moon" in Frame (shown on page 27): The design was stitched on a 15" square of Light Blue Aida (14 ct). Three strands of floss were used for Cross Stitch and 1 strand for Backstitch and French Knots. It was custom framed.

X	DMC	¼ X	B'ST	X	DMC	¼ X	B'ST	X	DMC	¼ X	X	DMC	
•	blanc			◎	745			✔*	840 &		•	310	French Knot
■	310				822				842		●	498	French Knot
■	321				838		✔	◈*	841 &				
	498			●*	839 &				842				
✖	744				840			+	3823				

* Use 2 strands of first floss color listed and 1 strand of second floss color listed.

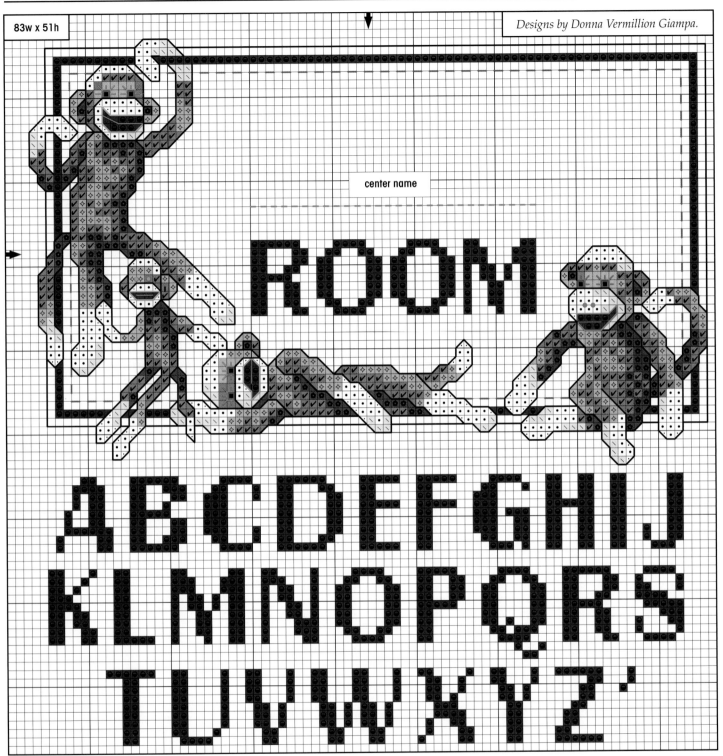

Designs by Donna Vermillion Giampa.

center name

ROOM

ABCDEFGHIJ
KLMNOPQRS
TUVWXYZ'

"Will's Room" Pillow (shown on page 26): The design was stitched on a 14" x 12" piece of Light Blue Aida (14 ct). Three strands of floss were used for Cross Stitch and 1 strand for Backstitch and French Knots. Personalize design using alphabet provided.

For pillow, you will need a 9" x 6½" piece of fabric for backing, a 31" length of ¼" dia. purchased cording with attached seam allowance, 13" length of ¼"w ribbon for hanger, and polyester fiberfill.

Centering design, trim stitched piece to measure 9" x 6½".

If needed, trim seam allowance of cording to ½". Pin cording to right side of stitched piece, making a ³⁄₈" clip in seam allowance of cording at corners. Ends of cording should overlap approximately 4". Turn overlapped ends of cording toward outside edge of stitched piece; baste cording to stitched piece.

Matching right sides and raw edges, pin stitched piece and backing fabric together. Leaving an opening for turning, use a ½" seam allowance to sew pillow front and backing fabric together. Trim seam allowances diagonally at corners; turn pillow right side out, carefully pushing corners outward. Stuff pillow with polyester fiberfill and blind stitch opening closed.

For hanger, refer to photo and tack each end of ribbon to each upper corner of pillow back.

73

ANGELS KEEP THEE

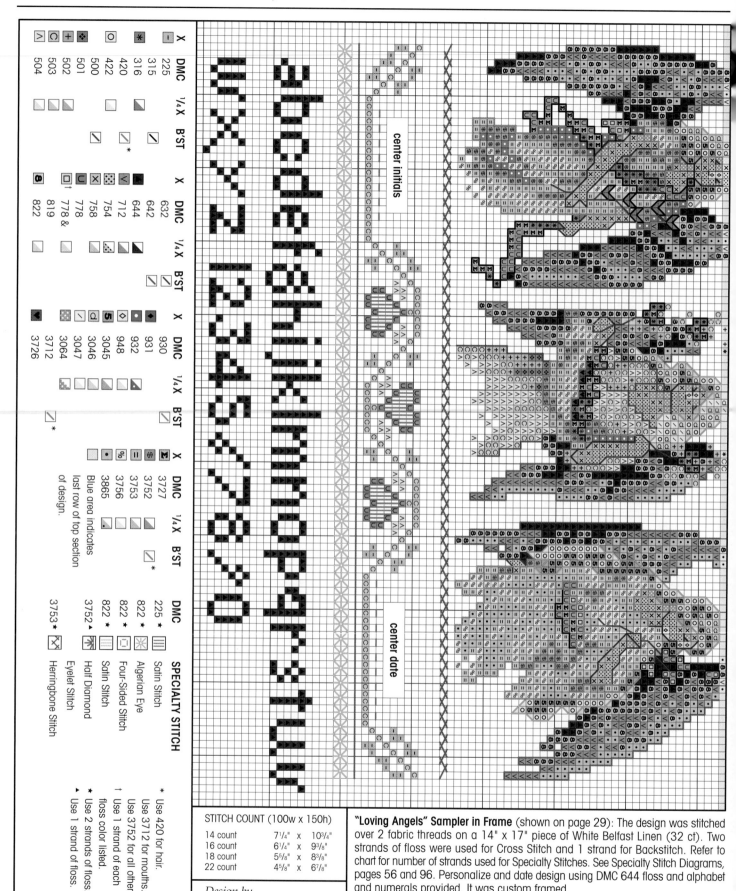

X	DMC	¼X	B'ST
⟨	225		
◯	315		
+	316		
◆	420		\ *
◯	422		
✳	500		
│	501		
	502		
	503		
	504		

X	DMC	¼X	B'ST
⊞	632		
▢	642		
⊠	644		
⊡	712		
⟨	754		
▦	758		
U	778		
◼	778 & 819		
	822		

X	DMC	¼X	B'ST
⊟	930		
◈	931		
◉	932		
	948		
▤	3045		
◆	3046		
⟨	3047		
▨	3064		
▣	3712		\ *
◼	3726		

X	DMC	¼X	B'ST
▥	3727 *		
●	3752 *		
◔	3753 *		
‖	3756		
M	3865		

SPECIALTY STITCH	DMC	
Satin Stitch	225 *	
Algerian Eye	822 *	
Four-Sided Stitch	822 *	
Satin Stitch	822 *	
Half Diamond	3752 ▲	
Eyelet Stitch	3752 ▲	
Herringbone Stitch	3753 *	

center initials

center date

Blue area indicates last row of top section of design.

abcdefghijklmnopqrstuvwxyz
1234567890

* Use 420 for hair.
Use 3712 for mouths.
Use 3752 for all other.
† Use 1 strand of each floss color listed.
★ Use 2 strands of floss.
▲ Use 1 strand of floss.

STITCH COUNT (100w x 150h)

14 count	7¼" x	10¾"
16 count	6¼" x	9⅜"
18 count	5⅝" x	8⅜"
22 count	4⅝" x	6⅞"

Design by Donna Vermillion Giampa.

"Loving Angels" Sampler in Frame (shown on page 29): The design was stitched over 2 fabric threads on a 14" x 17" piece of White Belfast Linen (32 ct). Two strands of floss were used for Cross Stitch and 1 strand for Backstitch. Refer to chart for number of strands used for Specialty Stitches. See Specialty Stitch Diagrams, pages 56 and 96. Personalize and date design using DMC 644 floss and alphabet and numerals provided. It was custom framed.

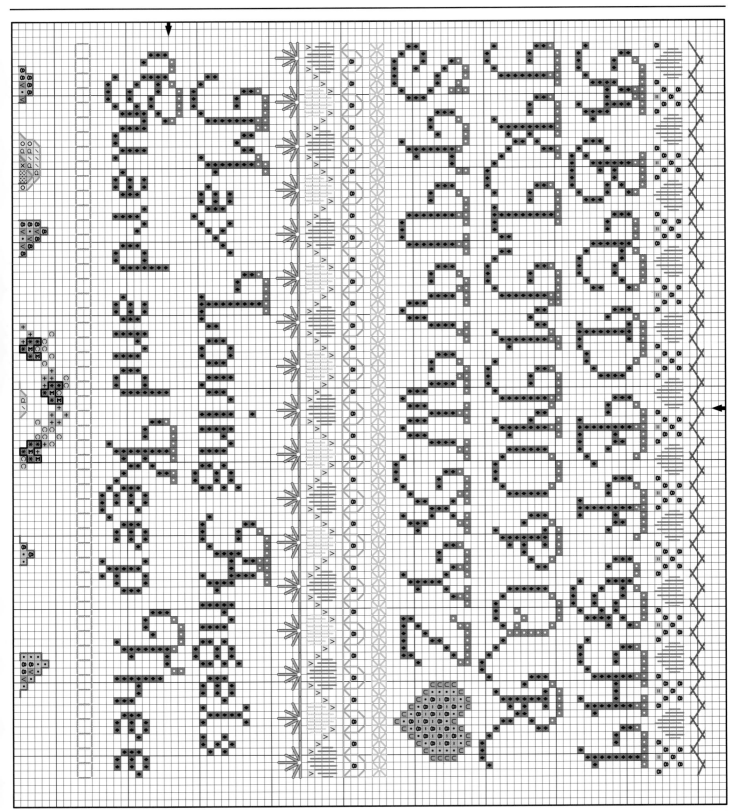

Angel Candle Tie (shown on page 28): A portion of the design (refer to photo) was stitched on a 6" x 7" piece of White Aida (14 ct). Two strands of floss were used for Cross Stitch and 1 strand for Backstitch.

For candle tie, you will need a 6" x 7" piece of lightweight white fabric for backing, fabric stiffener, small foam brush, 38" length of 2¼"w sheer wired ribbon, 38" length of 1⅞"w sheer ribbon, 8" length of ¼"w sheer ribbon, 4" dia. candle, and clear-drying craft glue.

To stiffen design, apply a heavy coat of fabric stiffener to wrong side of

stitched piece using a small foam brush. Matching wrong sides, place stitched piece on backing fabric, smoothing stitched piece while pressing fabric pieces together; allow to dry. Apply fabric stiffener to backing fabric; allow to dry. Cut out close to edges of stitched design.

Holding both 38" lengths of ribbon together and referring to photo, tie a bow around candle. Tie 8" length of sheer ribbon in a bow; referring to photo, glue stiffened design and bow to center of bow on candle. Trim all ribbon ends as desired.

VICTORIAN FANCIES

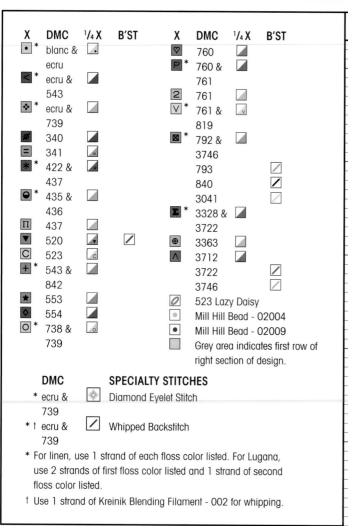

X	DMC	¼ X	B'ST		X	DMC	¼ X	B'ST
•*	blanc & ecru				♡	760		
◼<	ecru & 543				P*	760 & 761		
❖*	ecru & 739				2	761		
∅	340				V*	761 & 819		
=	341				⊠*	792 & 3746		
✳	422 & 437					793		
◖	435 & 436					840		
Π	437					3041		
▼	520				Σ*	3328 & 3722		
C	523				⊕	3363		
+ *	543 & 842				⋀	3712		
★	553					3722		
◆	554					3746		
O*	738 & 739				⊘	523 Lazy Daisy		
					·	Mill Hill Bead - 02004		
					•	Mill Hill Bead - 02009		

Grey area indicates first row of right section of design.

DMC	SPECIALTY STITCHES
* ecru & 739	☀ Diamond Eyelet Stitch
*† ecru & 739	⟋ Whipped Backstitch

* For linen, use 1 strand of each floss color listed. For Lugana, use 2 strands of first floss color listed and 1 strand of second floss color listed.

† Use 1 strand of Kreinik Blending Filament - 002 for whipping.

102w x 90h

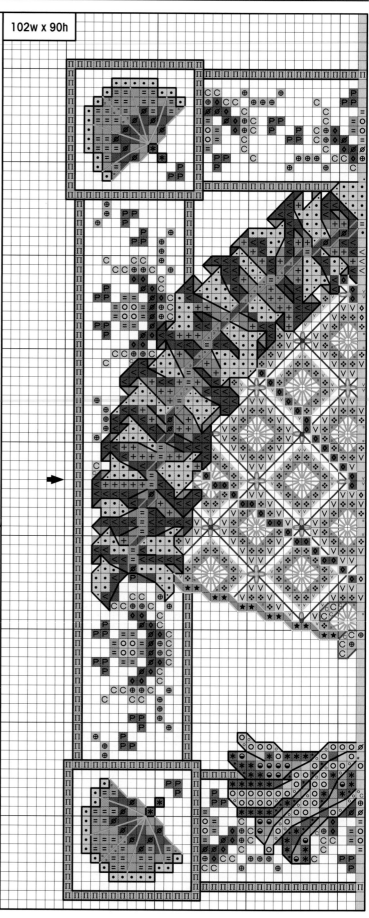

Victorian Fan in Frame (shown on page 31): The design was stitched over 2 fabric threads on a 15" square of Cream Cashel Linen® (28 ct). Two strands of floss were used for Cross Stitch and Lazy Daisy Stitch and 1 strand for Backstitch, unless otherwise noted in the color key. Refer to chart for type of thread and number of strands used for Specialty Stitches. See Specialty Stitch Diagrams, pages 56 and 96. Attach beads using 1 strand of DMC 760 floss for pink beads and 1 strand of DMC 341 floss for lavender beads. See Attaching Beads, page 95. It was custom framed.

Victorian Nosegay Shaker Box (shown on page 30): A portion of the design (refer to photo) was stitched over 2 fabric threads on an 8" x 7" piece of Cream Lugana (25 ct). Three strands of floss were used for Cross Stitch and 1 strand for Backstitch.

For Shaker box, you will need a 5" x 3½" oval Shaker box, 5" x 3½" oval piece of batting for lid, 2¾" x 14½" piece of fabric for box bottom, 15½" length of ⅝"w trim, tracing paper, pencil, fabric marking pencil, and clear-drying craft glue.

For pattern, trace around box lid onto tracing paper; add ¾" on all sides and cut out. Center pattern on wrong side of stitched piece; pin pattern in place. Use a fabric marking pencil to draw around pattern; remove pattern and cut out on drawn line. Clip ¼" into edge of stitched piece at 1" intervals. Glue batting on top of lid. Centering wrong side of stitched piece on batting; fold edges of stitched piece down and glue to side of lid. Referring to photo, glue trim to side of lid.

For box bottom, press fabric piece under ½" on short edges and ¼" on one long edge. Placing folded edge along bottom edge of box, glue fabric to box. Fold top edge of fabric to inside of box and glue in place.

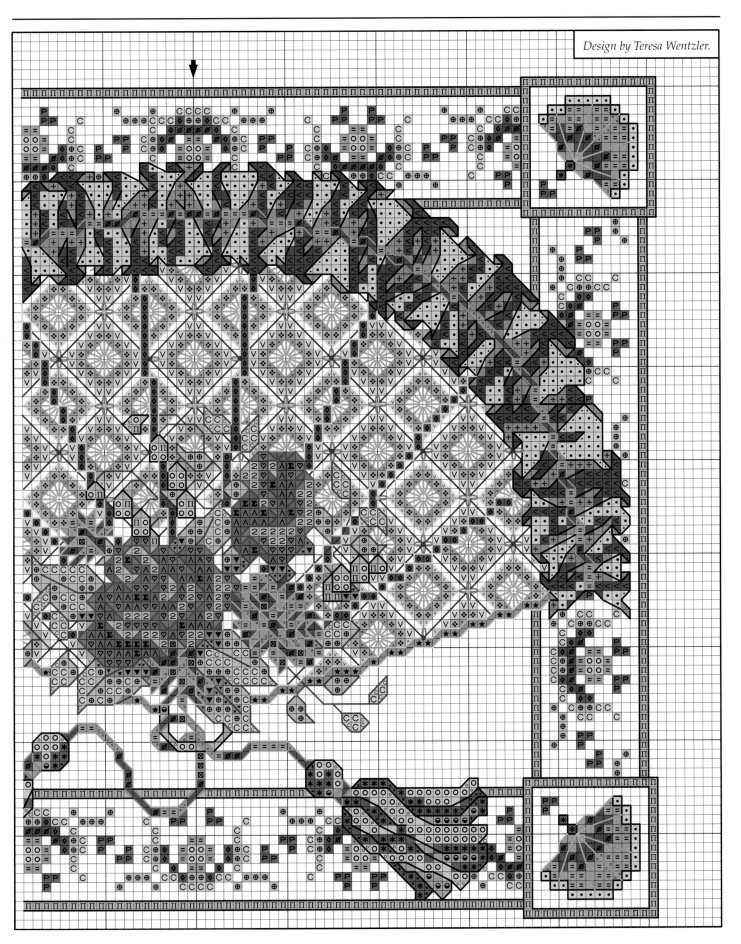

Design by Teresa Wentzler.

VICTORIAN FANCIES

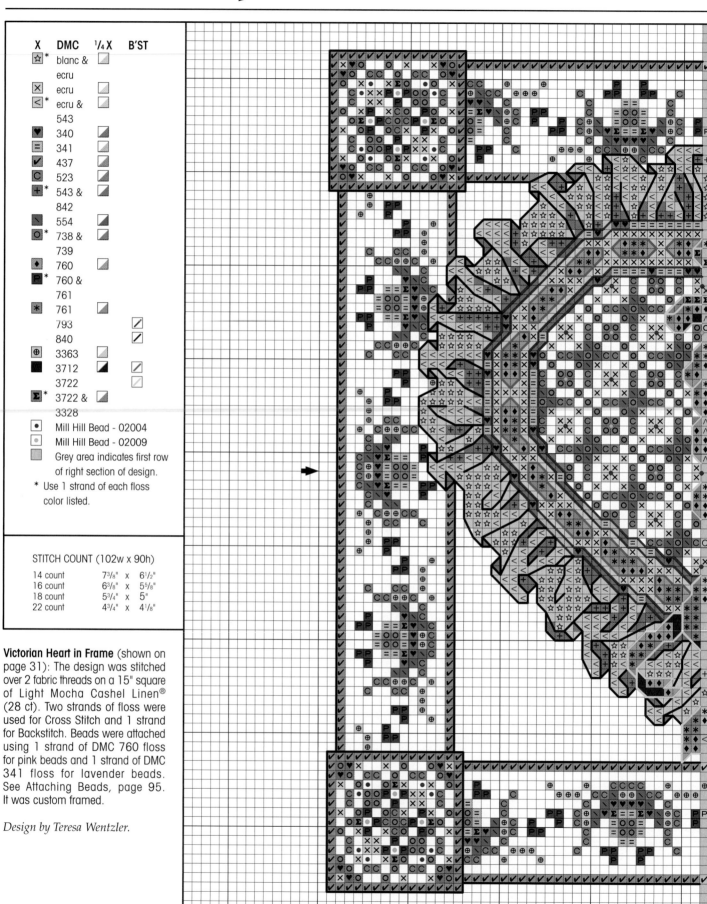

X	DMC	¼ X	B'ST
☆ *	blanc &		
	ecru		
✕	ecru		
< *	ecru &		
	543		
♥	340		
=	341		
✔	437		
C	523		
+ *	543 &		
	842		
◣	554		
O *	738 &		
	739		
◆	760		
P *	760 &		
	761		
✳	761		
	793		╱
	840		╱
⊕	3363		
■	3712		╱
	3722		╱
Σ *	3722 &		
	3328		
•	Mill Hill Bead - 02004		
•	Mill Hill Bead - 02009		
▧	Grey area indicates first row of right section of design.		

* Use 1 strand of each floss color listed.

STITCH COUNT (102w x 90h)

14 count	7³⁄₈"	x	6½"	
16 count	6³⁄₈"	x	5⅝"	
18 count	5¾"	x	5"	
22 count	4¾"	x	4⅛"	

Victorian Heart in Frame (shown on page 31): The design was stitched over 2 fabric threads on a 15" square of Light Mocha Cashel Linen® (28 ct). Two strands of floss were used for Cross Stitch and 1 strand for Backstitch. Beads were attached using 1 strand of DMC 760 floss for pink beads and 1 strand of DMC 341 floss for lavender beads. See Attaching Beads, page 95. It was custom framed.

Design by Teresa Wentzler.

special people

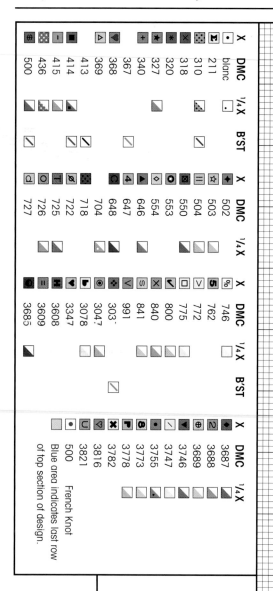

Color Key Table

X	DMC	1/4X	B'ST
	500		
	436		
	415		
	414		
	413		
	369		
	368		
	367		
	340		
	327		
	320		
	318		
	310		
	211		
	blanc		
	500		

X	DMC	1/4X	B'ST
	727		
	726		
	725		
	722		
	718		
	704		
	648		
	647		
	646		
	554		
	553		
	550		
	504		
	503		
	502		

X	DMC	1/4X	B'ST
	3685		
	3609		
	3608		
	3347		
	3078		
	3047		
	303		
	991		
	841		
	840		
	800		
	775		
	772		
	762		
	746		

X	DMC	1/4X
	3821	
	3816	
	3782	
	3778	
	3773	
	3755	
	3747	
	3746	
	3689	
	3688	
	3687	

500 — French Knot

Blue area indicates last row of top section of design.

STITCH COUNT (141w x 164h)

14 count	10 1/8" x 11 3/4"
16 count	8 7/8" x 10 1/4"
18 count	7 7/8" x 9 1/8"
22 count	6 1/2" x 7 1/2"

"A Mother's Love" in Frame (shown on page 33): The design was stitched over 2 fabric threads on a 17" x 18" piece of Antique White Belfast Linen (32 ct). Two strands of floss were used for Cross Stitch and 1 strand for Backstitch and French Knots. It was custom framed.

Design by Diane Brakefield.

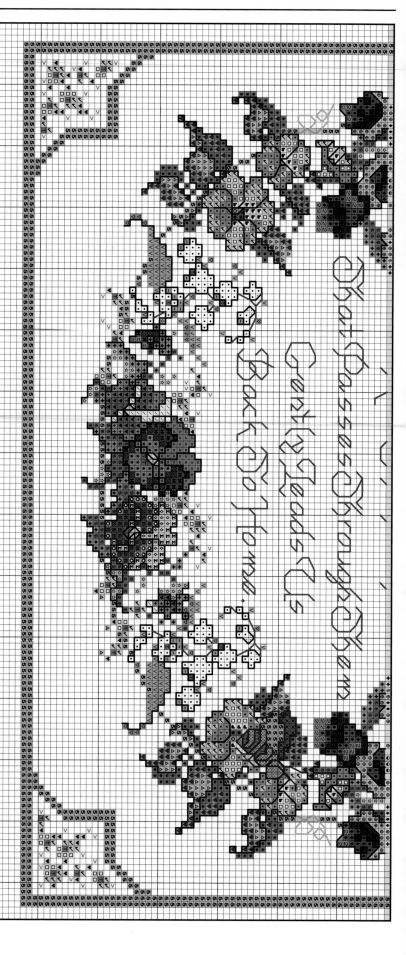

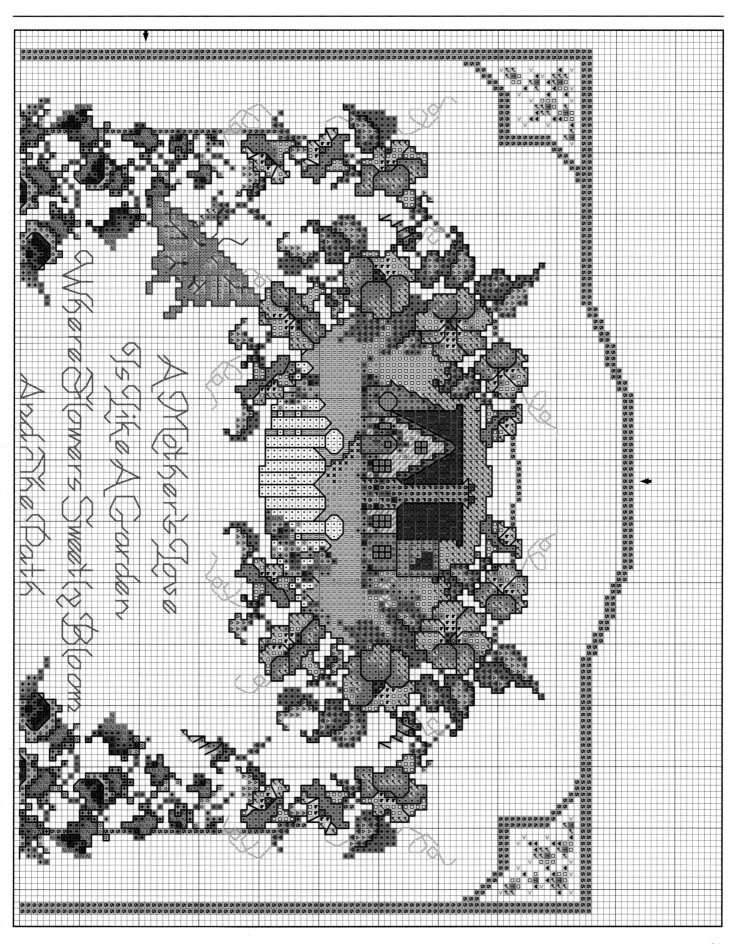

special people

STITCH COUNT (52w x 41h)

14 count	3³/₄"	x 3"
16 count	3¹/₄"	x 2⁵/₈"
18 count	3"	x 2³/₈"
22 count	2³/₈"	x 1⁷/₈"

X	DMC	B'ST
◆	367	
♡	368	
	413	╱
	414	╱
◓	500	╱
✳	503	
▢	504	
2	819	
▲	3685	
★	3687	
◇	3688	
✔	3689	

"Grandparents are Grand" in Frame (shown on page 32): The design was stitched over 2 fabric threads on 12" x 11" piece of Cream Cashel Linen® (28 ct). Two strands of floss were used for Cross Stitch and 1 strand for Backstitch. It was custom framed.

Design by Diane Brakefield.

FINISHING INSTRUCTIONS

Birth Sampler Pillow (shown on page 9, chart on page 49). For pillow, you will need an 11" x 8³/₄" piece of fabric for backing, 6" x 72" fabric strip for ruffle (pieced as necessary), and polyester fiberfill.

Centering design, trim stitched piece to measure 11" x 8³/₄".

For ruffle, press short edges of fabric strip ¹/₂" to wrong side. Matching wrong sides and long edges, fold strip in half; press. Machine baste ¹/₂" from raw edges; gather fabric strip to fit stitched piece. Matching raw edges, pin ruffle to right side of stitched piece overlapping short ends ¹/₄". Use a ¹/₂" seam allowance to sew ruffle to stitched piece.

Matching right sides and leaving an opening for turning, use a ¹/₂" seam allowance to sew stitched piece and backing fabric together. Trim seam allowances diagonally at corners; turn pillow right side out, carefully pushing corners outward. Stuff pillow with polyester fiberfill and blind stitch opening closed.

X	DMC	¼X	B'ST	X	DMC	¼X	B'ST	X	DMC	¼X	B'ST
•	blanc			∧	503	◨		■	938	◪	◿
≡	413	◨			632		◹	⬚	950	◪	
✔	414	◨		❖	738	◨		⬚	3064	◪	
	433	◨	◹	◿	739	◨			3750		◹
✚	434	◨		>	758	◨		⊥	3752	◻	
✖	435			■	839	◨	◹	▲	3772	◨	
○	436	◻		•	840	◪		✕	3773	◨	
▮	437	◨		%	841	◨		◇	3774	◨	
◕	500	◨	◹	∅	930	◨		◔	3778	◨	
‖	501	◨		♡	931	◨			3799		◹
C	502	◨		S	932	◨					

STITCH COUNT (83w x 97h)

14 count	6"	x	7"
16 count	5¼"	x	6⅛"
18 count	4⅝"	x	5½"
22 count	3⅞"	x	4½"

"Someone Special" in Frame (shown on page 34): The design was stitched over 2 fabric threads on a 14" x 15" piece of Raw Cashel Linen® (28 ct). Two strands of floss were used for Cross Stitch and 1 strand for Backstitch. It was custom framed.

Design by Donna Vermillion Giampa.

X	DMC	¼X	B'ST
•	blanc	•	/
◉	221	◢	
✔	223	◢	
O	224	◢	
	632		/
✳	640	◢	/
◆	642	◢	
2	644	◢	
⬚	754	⬚	
×	758	◢	
☆	760	◢	
+	822	◢	
★	838	◢	
⬛	839	◢	
•	840	•	
⊥	841	◢	
♥	902	◢	/
◻	930	◢	/
▼	931	◢	
C	932	◢	
✖	938		/
◇	948	◢	
⬚	3064	◢	
V	3722	◢	
8	3750		/
◡	3752	◢	
•	930	French Knot	

STITCH COUNT (57w x 68h)

14 count	4⅛"	x	4⅞"
16 count	3⅝"	x	4¼"
18 count	3¼"	x	3⅞"
22 count	2⅝"	x	3⅛"

"A Son Like You" in Frame (shown on page 35): The design was stitched over 2 fabric threads on a 12" x 13" piece of Raw Cashel Linen® (28 ct). Two strands of floss were used for Cross Stitch and 1 strand for Backstitch and French Knot. It was custom framed.

Design by Donna Vermillion Giampa.

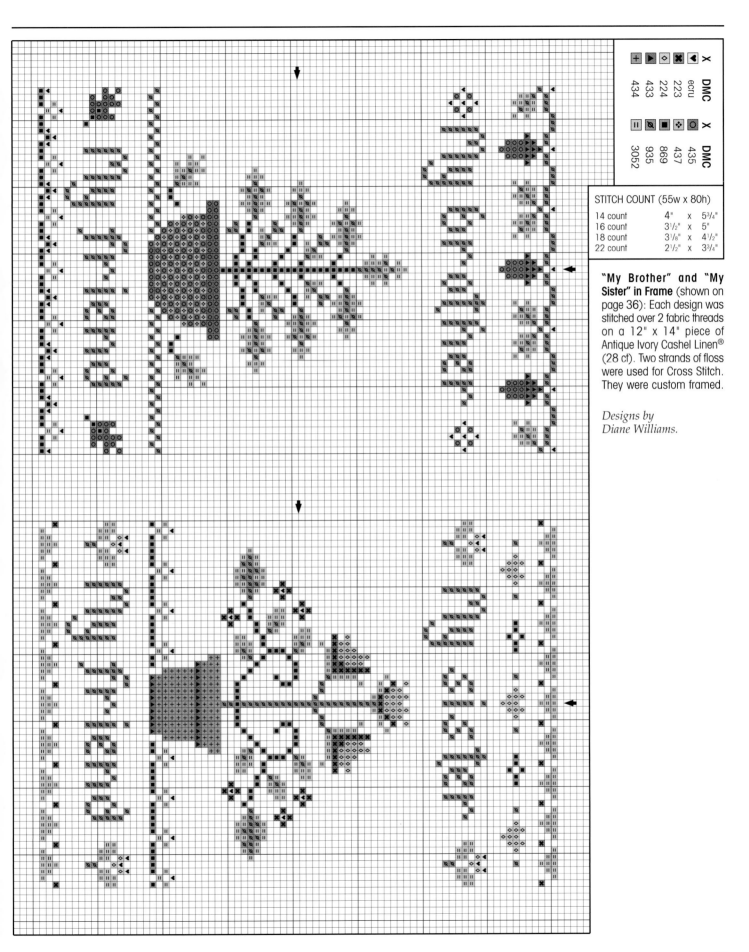

STITCH COUNT (55w x 80h)

14 count	4"	x	5³/₄"
16 count	3¹/₂"	x	5"
18 count	3¹/₈"	x	4¹/₂"
22 count	2¹/₂"	x	3³/₄"

"My Brother" and **"My Sister" in Frame** (shown on page 36): Each design was stitched over 2 fabric threads on a 12" x 14" piece of Antique Ivory Cashel Linen® (28 ct). Two strands of floss were used for Cross Stitch. They were custom framed.

Designs by Diane Williams.

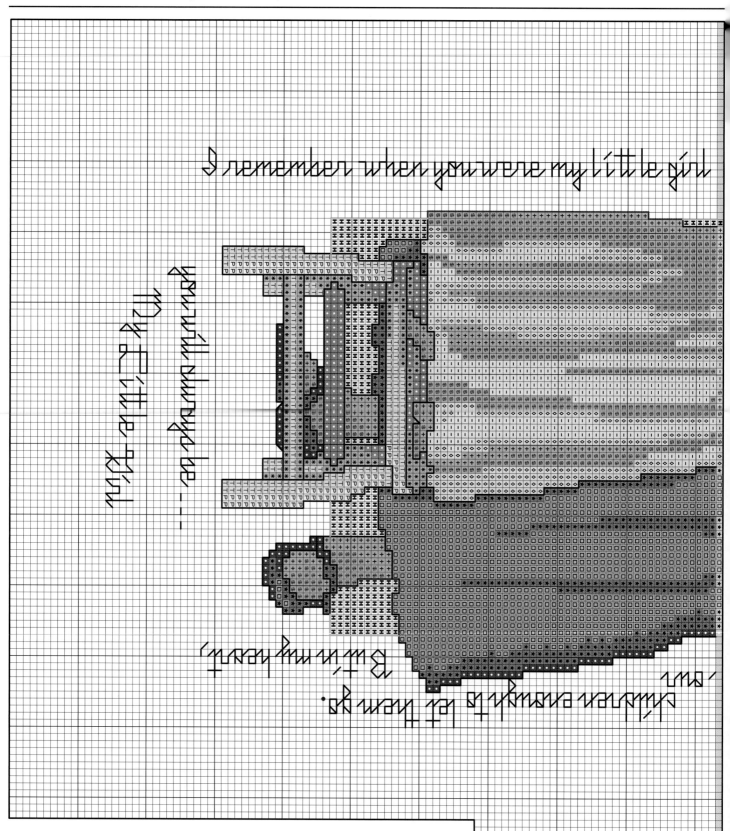

I remember when you were my little girl

"My Little Girl" in Frame (shown on page 37): The design was stitched over 2 fabric threads on a 14" x 20" piece of Cream Belfast Linen (32 ct). Two strands of floss were used for Cross Stitch and 1 strand for Half Cross Stitch, Backstitch, and French Knots. It was custom framed.

Design by D. Morgan.
Needlework adaptation by Carol Emmer.

STITCH COUNT (87w x 183h)

14 count	6¼"	x	13⅛"
16 count	5½"	x	11½"
18 count	4⅞"	x	10¼"
22 count	4"	x	8⅜"

DMC: blanc, 223, 224, 225, 333, 341, 352, 353, 407, 433, 435, 437, 501, 503, 611, 642, 644, 712, 739, 754, 758, 760, 794, 822, 839, 927, 948, 3072, 839

X   ¼X   ½X   B'ST

* Use 223 for all other.

Green area indicates last row of top section of design.

† Use 435 for hair, chin, and eyebrows. Use 794 for eyes. Use 224 for all other.

French Knot
Use 223 for top section of design.
Use 839 for all other.

FRIENDSHIP TOKENS

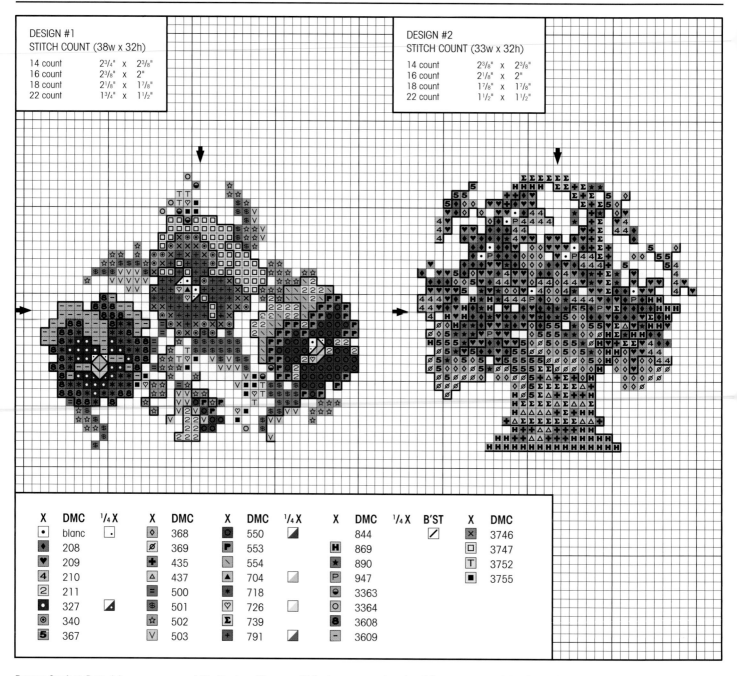

DESIGN #1
STITCH COUNT (38w x 32h)

14 count	2³/₄"	x	2³/₈"
16 count	2³/₈"	x	2"
18 count	2¹/₈"	x	1⁷/₈"
22 count	1³/₄"	x	1¹/₂"

DESIGN #2
STITCH COUNT (33w x 32h)

14 count	2³/₈"	x	2³/₈"
16 count	2¹/₈"	x	2"
18 count	1⁷/₈"	x	1⁷/₈"
22 count	1¹/₂"	x	1¹/₂"

X	DMC	¹/₄ X		X	DMC		X	DMC	¹/₄ X		X	DMC	¹/₄ X	B'ST		X	DMC
•	blanc	•		◇	368		◎	550	◸			844		◿		⊠	3746
◆	208			∅	369		P	553		H	869					▢	3747
♥	209			✚	435		\	554		★	890					T	3752
4	210			△	437		▲	704	◹	P	947					▪	3755
2	211			=	500		✳	718		◉	3363						
◙	327	◿		$	501		♡	726		○	3364						
◉	340			☆	502		Σ	739		⊗	3608						
5	367			V	503		+	791		-	3609						

Pansy Sachet Bag (shown on page 40): Design #1 was stitched over 2 fabric threads on a 7" x 9" piece of Platinum Cashel Linen® (28 ct). Two strands of floss were used for Cross Stitch and 1 strand for Backstitch.

For sachet bag, you will need a 4¹/₂" x 6" piece of Platinum Cashel Linen® for backing, 8" length of 1³/₄"w flat lace, polyester fiberfill, and scented oil.

Trim stitched piece to measure 4¹/₂" x 6", allowing ⁷/₈" margins at sides of design, 1" margin at bottom of design, and a 2³/₄" margin at top of design.

Matching right sides and leaving top edge open, use a ¹/₂" seam allowance to sew stitched piece and backing fabric together; trim seam allowances diagonally at corners. Turn top edge of bag ¹/₄" to wrong side and press; turn ¹/₄" to wrong side again and hem; turn bag right side out. Blind stitch straight edge of lace to top edge of bag. Stuff bag with polyester fiberfill. Place a few drops of scented oil on a small amount of fiberfill and insert in bag. Blind stitch top of bag closed.

Violet Basket, Floral Teacup, and Rose Bouquet Foundation Pieced Pillows (shown on page 41): Designs #2, #3, and #4 were each stitched over 2 fabric threads on a 10" square of Platinum Cashel Linen® (28 ct). Two

strands of floss were used for Cross Stitch and 1 strand for Backstitch.

For each foundation pieced pillow, you will need assorted fabrics for pillow top, a 10" square piece of fabric for backing, two 3¹/₂" tassels, assorted trims for embellishment, polyester fiberfill, tracing paper, and pencil.

For pattern, photocopy the Foundation Pieced Pattern, page 96, enlarging it 200%. Add ¹/₂" seam allowance on all four sides; cut out pattern. Your fabrics will be placed on the unmarked side of the paper and you will sew on the solid lines on the marked side of the paper. The numbers on the pattern indicate the order in which the fabric pieces are sewn.

For stitched piece, transfer pattern piece #1 onto tracing paper and cut out. Referring to photo, position pattern on wrong side of stitched piece; add ¹/₂" seam allowance to all sides of stitched piece and cut out. Position the stitched piece on the unmarked side of the pattern with the stitching right side out; pin in place.

Cut a piece of fabric for piece #2 at least ¹/₂" larger than pattern on all sides. Matching right sides and raw edges (**Fig. 1**), sew piece #2 to piece #1; trim seam allowance to ¹/₄". Flip piece #2 away from piece #1 and press. It will now cover #2 on the pattern (**Fig. 2**). Continue working in

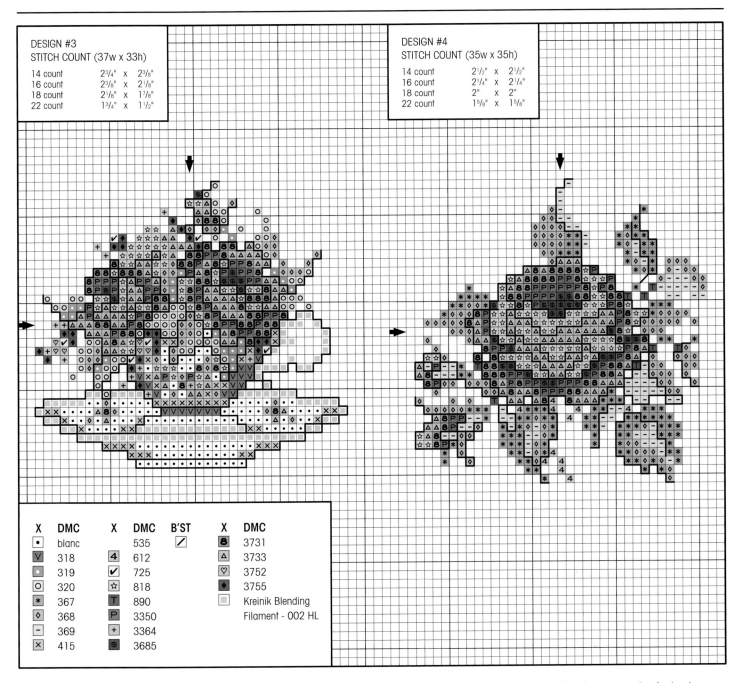

DESIGN #3
STITCH COUNT (37w x 33h)

14 count	2³⁄₄"	x	2³⁄₈"
16 count	2³⁄₈"	x	2¹⁄₈"
18 count	2¹⁄₈"	x	1⁷⁄₈"
22 count	1³⁄₄"	x	1¹⁄₂"

DESIGN #4
STITCH COUNT (35w x 35h)

14 count	2¹⁄₂"	x	2¹⁄₂"
16 count	2¹⁄₄"	x	2¹⁄₄"
18 count	2"	x	2"
22 count	1⁵⁄₈"	x	1⁵⁄₈"

X	DMC	X	DMC	B'ST	X	DMC
•	blanc		535	╱	8	3731
V	318	4	612		△	3733
•	319	✔	725		♡	3752
O	320	☆	818		◆	3755
*	367	T	890		▢	Kreinik Blending
◇	368	P	3350			Filament - 002 HL
-	369	+	3364			
✕	415	$	3685			

numerical order until block is completed. Trim pieced block to measure 10" square. Tear away paper and embellish pillow top with buttons, charms, lace, and ribbon as desired.

For pillow, matching right sides and leaving an opening for turning, use a ¹⁄₂" seam allowance to sew pillow top and backing fabric together. Trim seam allowances diagonally at corners; turn pillow right side out, carefully pushing corners outward. Stuff pillow with polyester fiberfill and blind stitch opening closed. Referring to photo, attach tassels at bottom corners.

Designs by Diane Brakefield.

Fig. 1

Fig. 2

BASKETS OF JOY

STITCH COUNT (93w x 88h)

14 count	6¾"	x 6⅜"
16 count	5⅞"	x 5½"
18 count	5¼"	x 5"
22 count	4¼"	x 4"

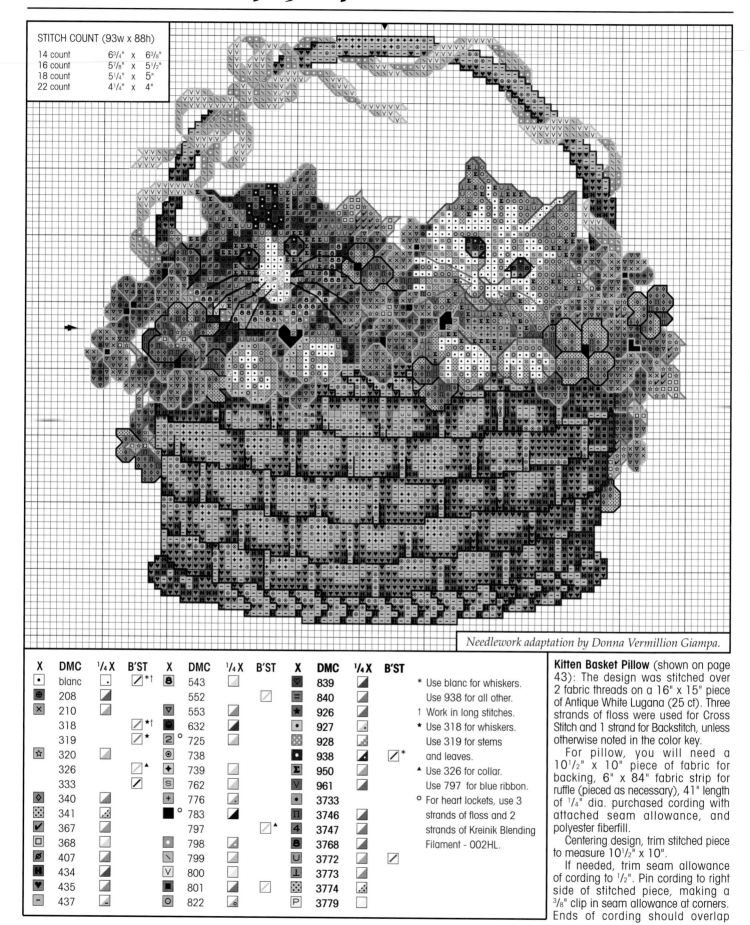

Needlework adaptation by Donna Vermillion Giampa.

X	DMC	¼ X	B'ST	X	DMC	¼ X	B'ST	X	DMC	¼ X	B'ST
•	blanc	•	⊘*†	8	543			▽	839		
⊕	208				552			≡	840		
⊠	210			▽	553			★	926		
	318		⊘*†	◨	632			•	927		
	319		⊘*	2	725	°			928		
☆	320			◉	738			◙	938		⊘*
	326		⊘▲	✦	739			Σ	950		
	333		⊘	S	762			V	961		
◇	340			+	776			•	3733		
⊡	341			■	783	°		Π	3746		
✔	367				797		⊘▲	4	3747		
▫	368			•	798			8	3768		
⊘	407			◡	799			U	3772		⊘
H	434			▽	800			⊥	3773		
♥	435			◼	801			⊡	3774		
−	437			○	822			P	3779		

* Use blanc for whiskers. Use 938 for all other.
† Work in long stitches.
★ Use 318 for whiskers. Use 319 for stems and leaves.
▲ Use 326 for collar. Use 797 for blue ribbon.
° For heart lockets, use 3 strands of floss and 2 strands of Kreinik Blending Filament - 002HL.

Kitten Basket Pillow (shown on page 43): The design was stitched over 2 fabric threads on a 16" x 15" piece of Antique White Lugana (25 ct). Three strands of floss were used for Cross Stitch and 1 strand for Backstitch, unless otherwise noted in the color key.

For pillow, you will need a 10½" x 10" piece of fabric for backing, 6" x 84" fabric strip for ruffle (pieced as necessary), 41" length of ¼" dia. purchased cording with attached seam allowance, and polyester fiberfill.

Centering design, trim stitched piece to measure 10½" x 10".

If needed, trim seam allowance of cording to ½". Pin cording to right side of stitched piece, making a ⅜" clip in seam allowance at corners. Ends of cording should overlap

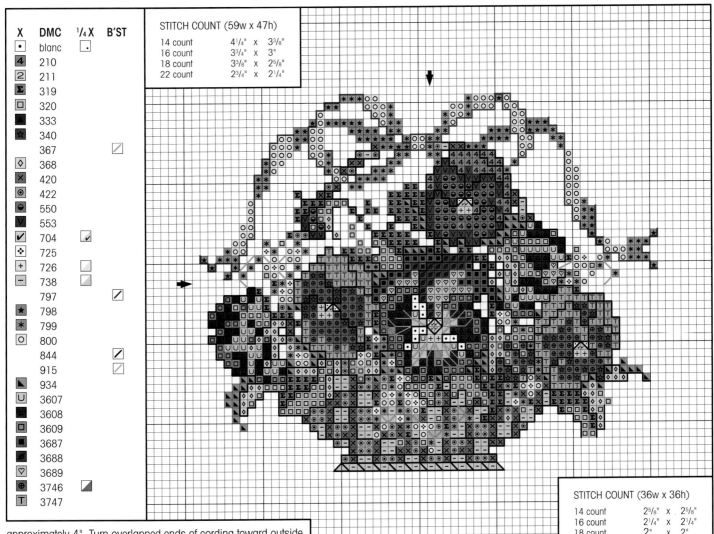

X	DMC	1/4 X	B'ST
·	blanc	·	
4	210		
2	211		
Σ	319		
□	320		
■	333		
☆	340		
	367		/
◇	368		
✕	420		
⊙	422		
⬠	550		
V	553		
✔	704	✔	
❖	725		
+	726	/	
−	738	/	
	797		/
★	798		
✳	799		
○	800		
	844		/
	915		/
◤	934		
U	3607		
■	3608		
□	3609		
■	3687		
⧄	3688		
♡	3689		
⊕	3746	◣	
T	3747		

STITCH COUNT (59w x 47h)

14 count	4 1/4"	x	3 3/8"
16 count	3 3/4"	x	3"
18 count	3 3/8"	x	2 5/8"
22 count	2 3/4"	x	2 1/4"

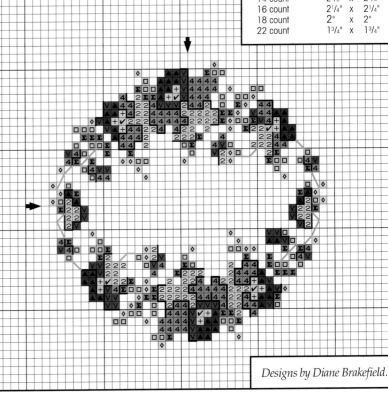

STITCH COUNT (36w x 36h)

14 count	2 5/8"	x	2 5/8"
16 count	2 1/4"	x	2 1/4"
18 count	2"	x	2"
22 count	1 3/4"	x	1 3/4"

approximately 4". Turn overlapped ends of cording toward outside edge of stitched piece; baste cording to stitched piece.

For ruffle, press short edges of fabric strip 1/2" to wrong side. Matching wrong sides and long edges, fold strip in half; press. Machine baste 1/2" from raw edges; gather fabric strip to fit stitched piece. Matching raw edges, pin ruffle to right side of stitched piece overlapping short ends 1/4". Use a 1/2" seam allowance to sew ruffle to stitched piece.

Matching right sides and leaving an opening for turning, use a 1/2" seam allowance to sew stitched piece and backing fabric together. Trim seam allowances diagonally at corners; turn pillow right side out, carefully pushing corners outward. Stuff pillow with polyester fiberfill and blind stitch opening closed.

Pansy Basket Doily (shown on page 42): The design was stitched on a purchased doily with a White Aida (14 ct) insert. Two strands of floss were used for Cross Stitch and 1 strand for Backstitch.

Pansy Wreath Pincushion (shown on page 42): The design was stitched on a 9" square of White Aida (14 ct). Two strands of floss were used for Cross Stitch and 1 strand for Backstitch.

For pincushion, you will need a purchased basket (3 1/2" x 2 1/2" opening) and polyester fiberfill.

Centering design, trim stitched piece to measure 8" x 7 1/2".

Baste around edges of stitched piece. Slightly gather stitched piece and stuff firmly with polyester fiberfill. Pull gathering thread tightly and secure. Referring to photo, insert stitched piece in basket.

Designs by Diane Brakefield.

cherished memories

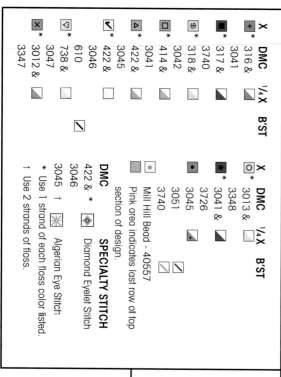

X	DMC	1/4X	B'ST
+ *	316 & 3041	◪	
■ *	317 & 3740	◪	
$ *	318 & 3042	◪	
□ *	414 & 3041	◪	
△ *	422 & 3045	◪	
✔ *	422 & 3046	◪	
	610		╱
♡ *	738 & 3047	◪	
× *	3012 & 3347	◪	
○ *	3013 & 3348	◪	
★ *	3041 & 3726	◪	
•	3045	◪	
	3051		╱
	3740		╱

◉ Mill Hill Bead - 40557

▢ Pink area indicates last row of top section of design.

DMC		SPECIALTY STITCH
422 & 3046 *	✺	Diamond Eyelet Stitch
3045 †	✳	Algerian Eye Stitch

* Use 1 strand of each floss color listed.
† Use 2 strands of floss.

STITCH COUNT (120w x 138h)			
14 count	8⅝"	x	9⅞"
16 count	7½"	x	8⅝"
18 count	6¾"	x	7¾"
22 count	5½"	x	6⅜"

Diamond Border Album (shown on page 39): The design was stitched over 2 fabric threads on a 17" x 18" piece of Platinum Cashel Linen® (28 ct). Two strands of floss were used for Cross Stitch and 1 strand for Backstitch. Refer to chart for number of strands used for Specialty Stitches. See Specialty Stitch Diagrams, page 56. Attach beads using 1 strand of DMC 842 floss. See Attaching Beads, page 95. To complete album, see Finishing Instructions, page 94.

Design by Teresa Wentzler.

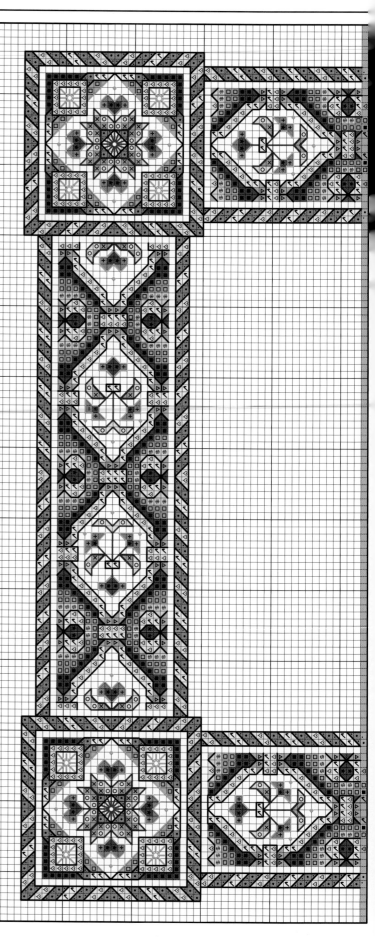

cherished memories

X	DMC	B'ST
V	3041	
◉	3045	
❈	3051	◿

DMC	SPECIALTY STITCHES
3012	⦀ Satin Stitch
3051	⦀ Satin Stitch

STITCH COUNT (57w x 79h)

14 count	4¹/₈"	x 5³/₄"
16 count	3⁵/₈"	x 5"
18 count	3¹/₄"	x 4¹/₂"
22 count	2⁵/₈"	x 3⁵/₈"

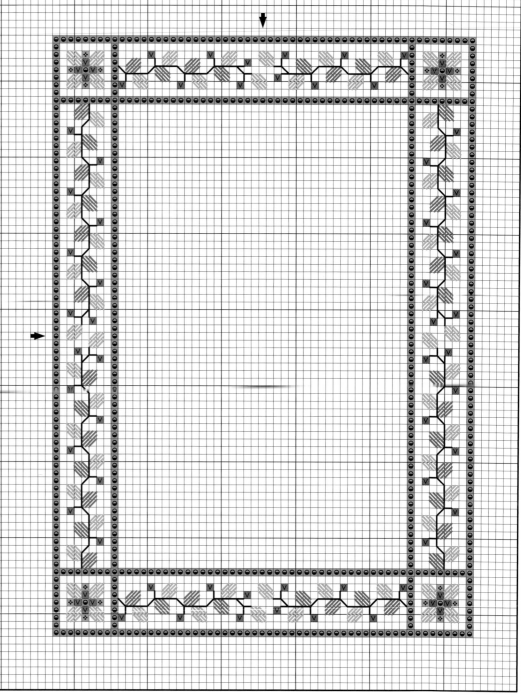

Floral Border Album (shown on page 38): The design was stitched over 2 fabric threads on a 12" x 14" piece of Platinum Cashel Linen® (28 ct). Two strands of floss were used for Cross Stitch and Satin Stitch and 1 strand for Backstitch. See Specialty Stitch Diagrams, page 96.

For album, you will need a 5" x 6¹/₂" photo album with a 2¹/₄" spine, ¹/₃ yard of 44"w fabric, 12¹/₂" x 6¹/₂" piece of batting for album, 4¹/₄" x 5³/₄" piece of batting for stitched piece, two 4¹/₂" x 6" pieces of poster board, 4¹/₄" x 5³/₄" piece of adhesive mounting board, tracing paper, pencil, and clear-drying craft glue.

From fabric, cut two 1¹/₂" x 6" pieces for spine strips, a 14¹/₂" x 8¹/₂" piece for album cover, and two 6¹/₂" x 8" pieces for inside covers.

FINISHING INSTRUCTIONS

Glue one long edge of one spine strip ¹/₄" under one long side of metal spine inside album; glue remaining edges of strip to album. Repeat with remaining spine strip and long side of metal spine; allow to dry.

For album cover, glue batting to outside of album. Center album, batting side down, on wrong side of fabric; fold fabric at corners to inside of album and glue in place. At center bottom of album, turn a 4" section of fabric ¹/₄" to wrong side (**Fig. 1**); glue folded edge under spine of album. Repeat at center top of album. Fold remaining edges of fabric to inside of album and glue in place; allow to dry.

Fig. 1

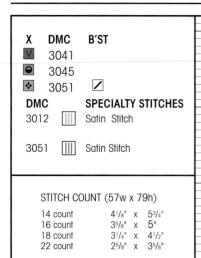

For inside cover, center one piece of poster board on wrong side of one piece of fabric; fold edges of fabric to back of poster board and glue in place. Glue wrong side of covered poster board to inside of front cover of album approximately ¹/₄" from top, bottom, and outside edges of album. Repeat with remaining piece of fabric and poster board for inside back cover.

For pattern, use tracing paper and draw around stitched piece close to inside and outside edges of design; cut out pattern. Draw around pattern once on mounting board and once on batting. Remove paper from mounting board and press batting piece onto mounting board.

For stitched piece, position pattern on wrong side of stitched piece; pin pattern in place. Cut stitched piece ¹/₂" larger than pattern on all sides. Clip ¹/₂" into stitched piece at corners. Center wrong side of stitched piece over batting on mounting board piece; fold edges of stitched piece to back of mounting board and glue in place.

Referring to photo, glue stitched piece to front of album at side and bottom edges.

Design by Teresa Wentzler.

GENERAL INSTRUCTIONS

WORKING WITH CHARTS

How to Read Charts: Each of the designs is shown in chart form. Each colored square on the chart represents one Cross Stitch or one Half Cross Stitch. Each colored triangle on the chart represents one One-Quarter Stitch or one Three-Quarter Stitch. In some charts, reduced symbols are used to indicate One-Quarter Stitches (**Fig. 1**). **Fig. 2** and **Fig. 3** indicate Cross Stitch under Backstitch.

Fig. 1   **Fig. 2**   **Fig. 3**

Black or colored dots on the chart represent Cross Stitch, French Knots, or bead placement. The black or colored straight lines on the chart indicate Backstitch. The symbol is omitted or reduced when a French Knot, Backstitch, or bead covers a square.

Each chart is accompanied by a color key. This key indicates the color of floss to use for each stitch on the chart. The headings on the color key are for Cross Stitch (**X**), DMC color number (**DMC**), One-Quarter Stitch (**¼X**), Three-Quarter Stitch (**¾X**), Half Cross Stitch (**½X**), and Backstitch (**B'ST**). Color key columns should be read vertically and horizontally to determine type of stitch and floss color. Some designs may include stitches worked with metallic thread, such as blending filament, braid, or cord. The metallic thread may be blended with floss or used alone. If any metallic thread is used in a design, the color key will contain the necessary information.

STITCHING TIPS

Working over Two Fabric Threads: Use the sewing method instead of the stab method when working over two fabric threads. To use the sewing method, keep your stitching hand on the right side of the fabric (instead of stabbing the fabric with the needle and taking your stitching hand to the back of the fabric to pick up the needle). With the sewing method, you take the needle down and up with one stroke instead of two. To add support to stitches, it is important that the first Cross Stitch be placed on the fabric with stitch 1-2 beginning and ending where a vertical fabric thread crosses over a horizontal fabric thread (**Fig. 4**). When the first stitch is in the correct position, the entire design will be placed properly, with vertical fabric threads supporting each stitch.

Fig. 4

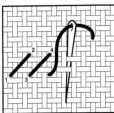

Attaching Beads: Refer to chart for bead placement and sew bead in place using a fine needle that will pass through bead. Bring needle up at 1, run needle through bead and then down at 2. Secure floss on back or move to next bead as shown in **Fig. 5**.

Fig. 5

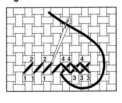

STITCH DIAGRAMS

Note: Bring threaded needle up at 1 and all odd numbers and down at 2 and all even numbers.

Counted Cross Stitch (X): Work one Cross Stitch to correspond to each colored square on the chart. For horizontal rows, work stitches in two journeys (**Fig. 6**). For vertical rows, complete each stitch as shown (**Fig. 7**). When working over two fabric threads, work Cross Stitch as shown in **Fig. 8**. When the chart shows a Backstitch crossing a colored square (**Fig. 9**), a Cross Stitch should be worked first; then the Backstitch (**Fig. 14** or **15**) should be worked on top of the Cross Stitch.

Fig. 6   **Fig. 7**

Fig. 8   **Fig. 9**

Quarter Stitch (¼X and ¾X): Quarter Stitches are denoted by triangular shapes of color on the chart and on the color key. For a One-Quarter Stitch, come up at 1 (**Fig. 10**), then split fabric thread to go down at 2. When stitches 1-4 are worked in the same color, the resulting stitch is called a Three-Quarter Stitch (**¾X**). **Fig. 11** shows the technique for Quarter Stitches when working over two fabric threads.

Fig. 10   **Fig. 11**

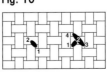   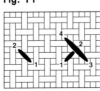

Half Cross Stitch (½X): This stitch is one journey of the Cross Stitch and is worked from lower left to upper right as shown in **Fig. 12**. When working over two fabric threads, work Half Cross Stitch as shown in **Fig. 13**.

Fig. 12   **Fig. 13**

Backstitch (B'ST): For outline detail, Backstitch (shown on chart and on color key by black or colored straight lines) should be worked after the design has been completed (**Fig. 14**). When working over two fabric threads, work Backstitch as shown in **Fig. 15**.

Fig. 14   **Fig. 15**

          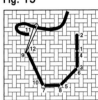

French Knot: Bring needle up at 1. Wrap floss once around needle and insert needle at 2, holding end of floss with non-stitching fingers (**Fig. 16**). Tighten knot, then pull needle through fabric, holding floss until it must be released. For larger knot, use more strands of floss; wrap only once.

Fig. 16

Lazy Daisy Stitch: Bring needle up at 1 and make a loop. Go down at 1 and come up at 2, keeping floss below point of needle (**Fig. 17**). Pull needle through and go down at 2 to anchor loop, completing stitch. (**Note:** To support stitches, it may be helpful to go down in edge of next fabric thread when anchoring loop.)

Fig. 17

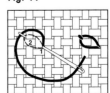

Continued on page 96.

FRIENDSHIP TOKENS

Violet Basket, Floral Teacup, and Rose Bouquet Foundation Pieced Pillows (shown on page 41, charts and instructions on pages 88-89).

Foundation Pieced Pattern

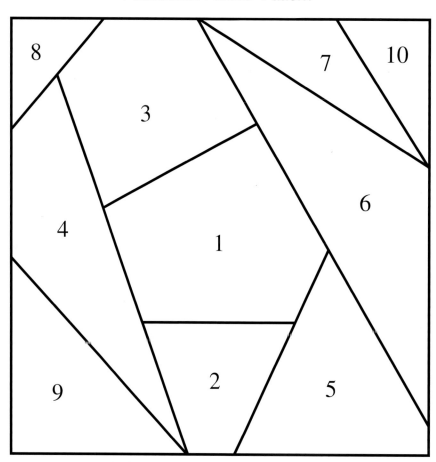

SPECIALTY STITCH DIAGRAMS
(continued from page 56).

Rhodes Stitch: This decorative stitch is formed by working eight stitches (stitches 1-16) as shown in **Fig. 9**.

Fig. 9

Satin Stitch: This stitch is a series of straight stitches worked side by side (**Fig. 10**). The number of threads worked over and the direction of stitches will vary according to the chart.

Fig. 10

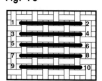

Whipped Backstitch: This stitch is formed by working a series of Backstitches (stitches 1-8) and then whipping these stitches with an alternate floss color starting at A and working towards B as shown in **Fig. 11**.

Fig. 11

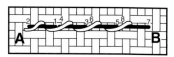

Instructions tested and photo items made by Arlene Allen, Lisa Arey, Alice Crowder, Muriel Hicks, Elizabeth James, Pat Johnson, Tammie Latimer, Phyllis Lundy, Kelly P. Magoulick, Patricia O'Neil, Dave Ann Pennington, Angie Perryman, Stephanie Gail Sharp, Anne Simpson, Lavonne Sims, Lorissa Smith, Helen Stanton, Trish Vines, Andrea Westbrook, and Sharon Woods.